# Student Workbook

## for

# Modern Media Writing

# Student Workbook
# for
# Modern Media Writing

**Rick Wilber**
*University of South Florida*

**Randy Miller**
*University of South Florida*

**WADSWORTH**
CENGAGE Learning·

Australia • Brazil • Japan • Korea • Mexico • Singapore • Spain • United Kingdom • United States

**WADSWORTH**
CENGAGE Learning™

**Student Workbook for Modern Media Writing**
Rick Wilber, Randy Miller

For product information and technology assistance, contact us at
**Cengage Learning Customer & Sales Support, 1-800-354-9706**

For permission to use material from this text or product,
submit all requests online at **www.cengage.com/permissions**
Further permissions questions can be emailed to
**permissionrequest@cengage.com**

ISBN-13: 978-0-534-52049-6

ISBN-10: 0-534-52049-9

**Wadsworth**
20 Channel Center Street
Boston, MA 02210
USA

Cengage Learning is a leading provider of customized learning solutions with office locations around the globe, including Singapore, the United Kingdom, Australia, Mexico, Brazil, and Japan. Locate your local office at **international.cengage.com/region**

Cengage Learning products are represented in Canada by Nelson Education, Ltd.

To learn more about Wadsworth, visit **www.cengage.com/wadsworth**
Purchase any of our products at your local college store or at our preferred online store **www.ichapters.com**

Printed in the United States of America
4 5 6 7 8        18 17 16 15 14

# CONTENTS

# PREFACE

This workbook is designed to complement the *Modern Media Writing* textbook and accompanying CD/ROM. What you will find here are exercises and activities designed to enable you to practice your skills at media writing. We expect that your instructor will also give you additional assignments based on the needs of each individual instructor.

Some of the exercises in this workbook are also found on the CD/ROM that came packaged with the *Modern Media Writing* textbook. However, we have included other activities in the workbook that are not found on the CD/ROM. Some CD/ROM activities, most notably the sound files designed to improve your note-taking ability, are not found in this workbook.

Additionally, the workbook includes summary material and key points from each chapter in *Modern Media Writing* and provides Internet websites for more information about the various chapter topics.

Your textbook authors would like to thank some folks who helped design activities for this workbook: our friend and colleague Kim Golombisky, who provided the activities in Chapter 12, and Charles McKenzie, the graduate student extraordinaire who helped provide activities in several chapters. We would especially like to thank our hard-working students at the University of South Florida: Tiffany Anderson, Chris Budzban, Kristan Bright, Megan Sullivan, Alexander Zesch and Jennifer Lefleur, who also provided activities.

We also thank our editor Holly Allen and Nicole George for providing guidance in finishing this workbook.

# Chapter 1
# Changing Definitions of the News

## Introduction:

The concept of what "news" is has changed over the centuries. Early newspapers were often censored by government, but by the early 1700s in the American Colonies independent editors were publishing whatever they thought was "news." During the 1800s the arrival of the Industrial Revolution brought large audiences for newspapers. By the 1920s radio had arrived with its own ideas of what was newsworthy, and by the 1950s television's rise changed the concept of news again.

Today, the different media each have their own ideas of what makes something newsworthy, with television most interested in dramatic and often live images, newspapers most interested personalities and the unusual, and magazines most interested in specific news relevant to their specialized audiences. Radio is most interested in sports and opinion, though some stations still provide timely coverage of breaking news.

## Key points:

- The idea of "news" varies from medium to medium.
- The idea of "news" has changed over time.
- The idea of "news" does have certain areas where the various media agree.
- The idea of "news" is changing again with the arrival of the Information Age.

And here are some places on the Internet where you can find about media history and news value:
http://www.nscee.edu/unlv/Colleges/Greenspun/Journalism_History/
http://www.mediahistory.com/
http://www.scripps.ohiou.edu/mediahistory/
http://www.newspapers.com

**Using InfoTrac College Edition,** you may enter the following terms for key word and subject searches: Free Speech, First Amendment, ethics in journalism within the following periodicals: American Journalism Review, Variety, Columbia Journalism Review.

# Activity 1.1

Decide which elements of newsworthiness are present in the following situations (careful, some may have no elements).

1. The President vetoes a bill cutting interstate highway funding.

2. The President poses for photographs with visiting college students from Germany.

3. The President poses for photographs with visiting college students from your university.

4. Your mayor, who is staunchly anti-crime, spent two months in a juvenile boot camp for committing a misdemeanor.

5. The city manager of Portland, Maine, resigns (unless you're from Maine, in which case the city manager is in Tucson, Ariz.).

6. The city manager of Portland, Maine, resigns after being arrested by federal agents for drug smuggling.

7. Your local Kiwanis Club holds a pancake breakfast fund-raiser.

8. Your local Kiwanis Club treasurer is arrested for embezzling pancake breakfast funds.

9. A man is murdered in Adelaide, Australia.

10. A man from your town is murdered in Adelaide, Australia.

11. The phone bill of John Smith, 1234 Oak Trail, will double next month.

12. The phone bill for everybody in your hometown will double next month.

13. The phone bill for everybody in Lubbock, Texas, will double next month (unless you're from Lubbock in which case, make it Ames, Iowa.)


14. Ben Atkins is coming to speak at your university. He is a criminology professor from across the country.


15. Actor Ben Affleck is coming to speak at your university.


## Activity 1.2

Early this morning, you unexpectedly hear that your company, McDole Limited, the largest employer in your town of 250,000, will today be bought by Gigantico Corp., a multinational corporation with headquarters in New York and London.

If you are a print reporter for the local newspaper, what are the most newsworthy facets of this story? What questions will you want to ask?

If you are a broadcast reporter for a local television station, what are the most newsworthy facets of this story? What else do you need beyond what the print reporter will get?

If you are a print reporter for a national newspaper like the New York Times, what are the newsworthy facets of this story? What questions will you want to ask?

If you are a print reporter for a national business news organization, such as the Wall Street Journal or Barron's, what are the newsworthy facets of this story? What questions will you want to ask?

If you are a broadcast reporter for a national broadcast news organization, like CNN or MS-NBC, what are the newsworthy facets of this story? What questions will you want to ask?

If you are working in public relations for McDole, what are the most newsworthy facets of the story? What will you need to emphasize in your releases?

If you are working in public relations for Gigantico, what are the most newsworthy facets of the story? What will you need to emphasize in your releases?

# Chapter 2
## Basic Structures for Media Writing

## Introduction:

Any communicator consciously chooses the order in which information is presented. The professional communicator chooses that order in the best way to reach that audience. For most news stories, writers will choose to structure information by its importance. In others, writers will construct the story chronologically. And in other cases, the writer will choose to use subject blocks as an organizing device.

As you improve as a communicator, you will want to master each of these story-telling forms. Then you can use them in different situations to most effectively reach your audience. There are more opportunities to practice these structures in Chapter 13's activities.

## Key points:

- The inverted pyramid is the most common form for news stories and, thus, a necessity to learn. It requires the reporters to begin with the most important information and then present information by its importance.

- The call-a-friend technique can help beginners determine the importance of different elements of the story.

- Most of the time, press releases should be written in inverted pyramid structure.

- Chronologies work when a strong narrative element is present. If a story builds to a climax, it may be a candidate to be presented chronologically.

- Hourglass and champagne-glass structures combine inverted pyramid structures with chronology.

- Key subject block structure allows writer to group information by subject. It is most effective in longer print stories and in broadcast writing.

Here are some important relevant websites where you can find more material on structures in writing: http://www.poynter.org/links (The Poynter Institute site has more than 200 links that can help writers.)

# Activity 2.1

This news story has been scrambled from its original form on pages 5 and 6.

You will need to locate the lead and then logically piece the story together from there. Remember that persons in news stories are referred to by full name on first reference. One strategy is to photocopy the assignment and cut the paragraphs into separate units. Or you might number them in the order that they should appear.

After moving to the area from Ohio, Hardigree and his two children were staying at the home of Charles Durand, 52, in Kissimmee at the time of the incident. _____

The girl said in her statement that she suffered "bruises, scratches and marks because of rope burns" when she was tied to the chair. The girl said in her statement "if you didn't call it child abuse, what was it?" _____

The girl asked in her statement for her father never to have contact with her again. The girl's brother is living with a foster family. _____

Michael Swindle, an attorney who represented Linda Durand, said the girl threatened to kill people and had emotional problems. _____

Referring to the actions of the father, Douglas Hardigree, 40, his daughter said in a statement read by her foster mother, "I'm your daughter and you treated me like an animal." _____

Hardigree will serve less than 20 months in prison. Hardigree was given credit for more than two and a half months of time served in county jail. _____

Durand's daughter, Linda, was sentenced to one year in jail by Circuit Court Judge Frank N. Kaney. Linda Durand, who was 19 when the girl stayed at the home, was given credit for 54 days in jail. _____

The father of a 12-year-old girl who was made to sleep nightly tied up on a lounge outside a home on Saber Court received 22 months in prison when he was sentenced on Friday. _____

During the trial, the brother told jurors that his sister was frequently tied up as a form of discipline. He said he was afraid of his sister and feared she could hurt him.

None of the defendants elected to speak for themselves before sentencing, at which the girl's mother and her foster mother were angered by a pre-sentencing report that recommended probation for the defendants.

Kaney also referred to the girl's emotional problems prior to sentencing Hardigree.

"But instead of trying to resolve them," the judge said about the girl's problems, "he had her tied up in a lawn chair."

The girl's foster mother read a statement condemning her father's treatment of her. The father and two residents of the home were arrested on charges of aggravated child abuse last April.

## Activity 2.2

Again, we have a case of a news story being scrambled on pages 7 through 9. In this case, you should see whether you can structure the story in more than one way - can you use a form other than an inverted pyramid in piecing this story together? If not, can you structure the story so that a different angle is featured at the top of the pyramid? What changes would you have to make to accommodate that new lead?

Right now, there are about 2,978 people who live in Narcoossee and close to 1,000 students who attend Narcoossee Community School. _____

Right now, the fire station on Narcoossee Road is staffed by volunteers. _____

Jim DiGiacomo, principal at Narcoossee, said he has had several parents express their concerns about not having a full-time paramedic in the area. _____

Because these stations are not located in Narcoossee, the average rescue response time into Narcoossee is 13 minutes and 49 seconds. The average response time for all of Osceola County is 10 minutes and 33 seconds. _____

Having a paramedic in Narcoossee from 8 a.m. to 5 p.m. Monday through Friday would cost the county $65,460 through October. Offering paramedic coverage 24 hours a day in the area would cost the county $269,400. _____

"Anything they can give us is great," DiGiacomo said. "But we still want a paramedic in the area." _____

Tammie Mullins, a parent of three children who attend Narcoossee Community School, said that she hopes the county will continue to work toward having full-time fire and rescue workers located in the Narcoossee area. _____

This will be beneficial in determining if the Narcoossee area has the greatest need in the county for a fully-staffed fire station, Hoang added.

"Now is the time that we need to address increasing coverage for the fringe areas. That's what we're trying to work toward," Dunnick said.

Osceola County officials are working toward forming an interlocal agreement with St. Cloud to provide first response fire and rescue services to the Narcoossee area.

"We have some concerns about that," DiGiacomo said. "I would rather not think of a student or a teacher being injured ... and then waiting 15 minutes for an ambulance."

"We want to enter into an agreement with St. Cloud so they'll be able to respond immediately to a call," said County Commissioner Chuck Dunnick.

Currently, fire and rescue workers from the fire stations on Deer Run Road, in Buenaventura Lakes and in St. Cloud serve as back-ups to the volunteers.

Entering into an agreement with St. Cloud would be the first step in working toward hiring a full-time paramedic in Narcoossee during school hours and eventually offering full-time paramedic coverage 24-hours a day, Dunnick said.

County officials are in the process of forming a master plan for the county that would include a list of locations that are in need of a fully staffed fire station, said Twis Hoang, public information officer for the county.

The paramedics were from the Buenaventura Lakes fire station, which is about 15 minutes away, DiGiacomo said.

One of DiGiacomo's concerns is that if the county enters into an agreement with St. Cloud that it will stop there.

This year there have been two incidents including a traffic accident in front of the school and a student who was injured that required a paramedic, DiGiacomo said.

Don Adams, emergency services director, could not be reached for comment by deadline.

Several parents of children who attend Narcoossee Community School have been concerned since the school opened last year that there is not a full-time paramedic in Narcoossee during school hours.

"Seven minutes is helpful and I hope they can form the agreement," Mullins said. "But this area is growing so rapidly ... they need to look at placing someone out here full-time."

By entering into an interlocal agreement with St. Cloud, the average response time into Narcoossee would be 7 minutes and 14 seconds and it would be at no cost to the county.

## Activity 2.3

You don't have to find the lead here. We've already placed it at the top of the story. But the order of other paragraphs is scrambled. Using what you have learned about story structures, place the remaining information in order. Is there only one way to make the information fit after the lead? If you can find more than one option, which one works better? Why?

**CAPE CANAVERAL - One of NASA's most successful recent missions ended Monday with an unprecedented landing on an asteroid more than 196 million miles from Earth.**

The spacecraft, launched Feb. 17, 1996 from Cape Canaveral Air Force Station, sent a bonanza of photos and readings to scientists as it orbited the 22-mile-long Eros. It took about 160,000 snapshots of the surface of the asteroid and beamed back more than 11 million readings from its other instruments.

_____

Congratulations flowed in from above Earth, as well. Atlantis astronaut Tom Jones was performing a space walk when Mission Control told the crew of the near-perfect landing.

_____

Eros has about 1/1,000 the gravity of Earth, so the small jets on NEAR would be able to lift it off the surface.

_____

"I am happy to report that the NEAR has touched down," Project Manager Robert Farquhar said to cheers from scientists at the Johns Hopkins University Applied Physics Laboratory in Maryland. "We are getting signals (from the surface of the asteroid)."

_____

Just minutes after the 9-foot-long spacecraft hit the surface, antennas on Earth picked up radio signals indicating it was still alive.

_____

But after flying above the asteroid since Feb. 14, 2000, project managers at Johns Hopkins University's Applied Physics Laboratory decided to get some "bonus science" out of the mission. That meant steering the satellite down to the surface in a controlled impact.

_____

(more)

10

The maneuver gave researchers their closest look at the space rock, showing details just inches across.

There was no word on what position the probe was in when it landed, but scientists were encouraged that the signals from it got stronger after landing.

As it approached the surface of the asteroid at about the speed of a parachutist, NEAR returned photos of a relatively craterless area strewn with large boulders and smaller rocks. Scientists hope to use the last few photos to determine whether the asteroid is covered with rocks or soil, as well.

Before the NEAR landing, Farquhar said the spacecraft would not reveal any new science data once on the asteroid's surface because the main antenna would be blocked. The spacecraft, which has rechargeable batteries, could stay alive for months because its solar panels would be facing the Sun.

The craft was low on fuel and all of its scientific goals were met when project managers at Johns Hopkins decided to land on the asteroid.

The satellite was built to orbit the 4-billion-year-old Eros taking pictures and readings that would give scientists insights into the construction of some of the oldest objects in the solar system.

"It's really an amazing place for our spacecraft to be," Jones said. "I hope we have some astronauts following to the asteroid in just a few years."

The $223 million NEAR mission, for Near Earth Asteroid Rendezvous, was never intended to land - it was designed only to orbit the 21-mile-long Eros asteroid taking pictures and sending back readings.

It was the first time anyone landed a spacecraft on an asteroid. The NEAR experiment also marked the first time controllers have tried to land a machine that was never meant to land.

(more)

11

The university, which built the spacecraft, has been operating the mission for NASA.

_____

Jones formerly studied asteroids for the Central Intelligence Agency and NASA before joining the astronaut corps.

_____

However, the easy landing inspired confidence in spacecraft controllers. They could decide to use the NEAR's rockets again to skip the satellite off the asteroid a few hundred feet and land somewhere else, taking more pictures along the way.

_____

## Activity 2.4

From the following information, write a five-sentence inverted pyramid story, being sure to put the most important information in the first sentence, the second most information in the second sentence, etc.

Who: Bishop Xavier Roman of the archdiocese of Harbinger.

Why: Selected because of a 23-year stint leading charity work for the state's underprivileged and other civic activities.

Where: The Founders' Day parade begins at the corner of Stovall Boulevard and Norsworthy Avenue and finishes in the City Square with speeches by the mayor and the parade marshal.

How: The Harbinger Chamber of Commerce annually selects the parade marshal.

What: Roman is the grand marshal for the 94th Founders' Day parade in Harbinger on the first of next month. All Harbinger schoolchildren are given the day off and a large celebration takes place downtown.

## Activity 2.5

Write a brief news story in inverted pyramid style from the following news release but be careful, this is not a particularly well-written release in style and format.

WE ALL SCREAM FOR ICE CREAM!

Jack and Diane's Ice Cream Shoppe will be the very proud sponsers of the first annual Harbinger Ice Cream Eating Championship. There will be 3 divisions at the event: kids, teen-agers and adults. Jack and Diane's have decided to host the event at Harbinger Elms Mall Saturday at 12:00 noon on June 21, which is the longest day of the year, according to the calendar.

Anyone interested in participating in the contest should contact Jack and/or Diane at their shop at 3707 Jolliffe Avenue. There is a form to fill out and a medical waiver to be signed by all competitors. Jack and Diane Bleske are co-owners of the popular ice cream eatery.

All potential eaters will have 10 minutes to eat as much savory Jack and Diane's ice cream as they can. The winner will be the one to completely finish the most containers of Uncle Gene's Vanilla Bean ice cream within the allotted time. Kids will compete by eating Gooey Purple Vanilla ice cream.

Jack and Diane's is the only locally owned ice cream to have placed in the Top 20 nationally in the prestigious Golden Scoop awards presented by the National Dessert Makers Association, which consists of restauranteurs and professional chefs who specialize in desserts. The Bleskes have placed in the Top 20 for the last 4 years.

# Chapter 3
# Grammar or Style Trouble Spots

## Introduction

The basics of grammar and style are important. They are the building blocks you use to write your stories in a way that readers can clearly understand. Also, basic skills like spelling, capitalization, punctuation, noun/pronoun and noun/verb agreement must be under your control before you can move on to more complex writing skills.

Many beginning media writers seem to have particular problems with certain matters of usage and a number of common errors. These kinds of mistakes are red flags for editors and you'll want to avoid them.

## Key Points

- Good spelling is essential, and you're spellchecker isn't always write so you can't trust it.

- "It's" can be used only as the contraction for "it is."

- Every student learns they must make their nouns and pronouns agree.

- Sloppy writing tells editors that you can't be trusted.

- A number of style issues are different for media writers than for academic writers.

- Within media writing, too, there are occasional style differences between broadcast, newspaper, magazine, public relations and advertising. You must learn which is appropriate for your field or for your publication.

**Using InfoTrac College Edition**, you may enter the following terms for key word and subject searches: Free Speech, First Amendment, ethics in journalism within the following periodicals: American Journalism Review, Variety, Columbia Journalism Review.

# Activity 3.1

Boring verbs leads to boring copy. Give these verbs a little pick-me-up, and look out for the style errors that appear here.

1. The Wellington Police Department received over a dozen calls last night about strange aircraft that they said they saw hovering West of the city.

2. A convenience store received damage last night when an off-duty Harbinger police officer accidentally drove his squad car through the window and into the refrigerated stockroom of the store.

3. Rush-hour motorists on Busch Blvd. faced a 45-minute delay yesterday when the roadway was blocked by an overturned beer truck

-- Insert hyphens and close up compound words.

4. Although the mayor said the counterproposal was a "well intentioned cure all," she said it would not immediately affect the 12 year old deficit.

5. A part time maintenance worker will be hired to fix the vending machines that are out of order.

6. Out of state motorists will pay an additional $10 for double parked vehicles. The additional revenue will fund a new band shell, firetruck and weight lifting center.

7. The walk on wide receiver's goalline catch ended the Bulls' come from behind victory over the twice beaten Rams. The jubilation was short lived though. On the ensuing point after attempt, the place kicker missed the goal posts and sprained his ankle.

8. The two car accident left a 10 mile back up on the inter state.

## Activity 3.2

Determine whether a quote or a paraphrase works better in these examples with three options. Be prepared to explain why you might make your case.

1a. Beau Knight said, "I don't know. I guess that the best way to describe my emotions right now is that I am jubilant. Our team just refuses to lose."

1b. A jubilant Beau Knight said, "Our team just refuses to lose."

1c. Beau Knight said he was jubilant and that his team refuses to be beaten.

2a. The city's only ambulance is 14 years old, the chief said.

2b. "That ambulance is 14 years old," the chief said. "It's the only one in the city."

2c. Referring to the 14-year-old ambulance, the chief said, "It's the only one in the city."

## Activity 3.3

This exercise gives you practice in using quotation marks. Direct quotations are underlined. Please correctly use quote marks.

The skies over Argentina are beautiful the 13-year-old pilot said, I can't wait to fly there again

I hope we never have to face this again the governor said but if we do we'll be more prepared.

The events of Sept. 11 have profoundly changed the nation said the speaker. She added that people will just have to live with the changes.

In this sentence, the section in bold is a quotation within a quotation. Insert the proper quotation marks.

She told me **I didn't vote for the plan** but I think she did Dillon said.

## Activity 3.4

Please find a specific phrase or phrases for these vague descriptions.

several days ago             _____

inexpensive plan       .      _____

local elected official        _____

a family's dog               _____

federal program             _____


## Activity 3.5

Please tighten the following lead.

State appeals judge Donald Stevens announced yesterday at 11:13 p.m. at his office in the Wellington courthouse that he was denying the allegations made by Marco Blanco, owner of Wellington's Brown Bag grocery store, that the judge had been biased in his ruling against the store because the judge owns a meat-packing plant.

# Activity 3.6

Please eliminate the redundancies from the following passage.

At 8:15 a.m. this morning, the 2-week-old baby still remained in critical condition. Every single second, her parents remained by her side, but they had not been allowed to hold their daughter for a period of ten days.

As a consequence of her birth defect, she had a need for constant care and was completely surrounded by medical equipment. Her mother had assembled together the best doctors in the state. Even during the night hours, this team remained engaged in checking the various machines that served the purpose of monitoring the baby. One night, all of a sudden, an alarm sounded.

One of the dangers for journalistic writers is the overuse of passive voice. In the story below, find passive voice and change it when it improves the sentence.

A decision was made by a Harbinger County grand jury Thursday in Superior Court. Veteran Mansfield police officer Dave Snavely was found guilty of manslaughter charges.

He was made by the ruling the first Mansfield cop in more than a decade to be charged with a killing.

Snavely, 48, was charged with shooting a man during a brawl at a Harbinger bar last year.

The testimony of several witnesses was that Snavely, a 19-year veteran, had been drinking tequila shots for three hours before the shooting as the bar closed.

Snavely was charged with shooting 27-year-old surveyor John Custis at Rum Point Bar in Harbinger's bar district. Custis was shot once in the stomach and died less than an hour later.

According to witnesses, the bar fight was initiated when Custis and another patron began punching each other after Custis said the man looked like Mick Jagger. When the fight was continuing outside, Custis, who was punched four times in the face, was able to run to his pickup truck and was able to grab a metal theft-protection device.

Snavely was moving to his Toyota where he was able to grab his police-issue semiautomatic pistol.

Several witnesses were saying that Snavely was identifying himself as a police officer and was able to shoot as Custis was approaching him. Others were saying that Snavely never was identifying himself and was shooting without warning.

Bartender Natalie Grossberg was able to tell the court that she had served Snavely about a dozen tequila shots. But police were unable to confirm her story since they did not give Snavely a breathalyzer test.

# Activity 3.7

Correct the agreement problems in the sentences below. Be careful, not every sentence has a problem.

The University of South Florida has quadrupled their on-campus dorms in the last five years.

When a student violates the university's honor code, they will face a hearing that can recommend expulsion.

When the agency's director knows a candidate for inclusion, he or she must let the selection committee know in advance.

The Baltimore Ravens won their first Super Bowl in 2001. Baltimore won their first World Series in 1966.

Education, of all of the state's problems, are not being responded to correctly, the poll says.

IBM announced that they would reduce their workforce by 3,000 workers next week.

Tom Hanks and Meg Ryan is the quintessential on-screen couple.

The quartet sang their signature number, "Birdland," to open the show.

The quartet sang their newest hits to close the show.

Wilber and Miller have written its textbook for the introductory college writing class.

Auburn will get the football at their own 20-yard line.

## Activity 3.8

Correct any sentences that may have misplaced modifiers or shifts in person, place or time.

Running wildly down the lane, the accident was unavoidable.

As the businessman greeted the clergyman as Gretchen noticed that his breath smelled of alcohol.

Waving his baton wildly, the band director tried to get our attention.

If the students have difficulty finding a parking space, you should get to class earlier.

Becky received an A in physics while his performance in calculus was below par because of my instructor.

## Activity 3.9

Correct the misuse of these misused words and phrases. Not every sentence has problems, however.

Hopefully, we won't march behind the Budweiser wagon in the parade.

She said hopefully, maybe the blind date will turn out to be handsome and nice.

The 112th Rose Bowl parade was a unique occurrence.

The new surgical procedure is sort of unique, the doctor said.

He blushed a livid red.

His new novel literally blew my head off.

The season conclusion of "West Wing" figuratively sent shivers up and down my spine.

The Dixie Chicks are an awfully talented group of musicians.

Bob never listens to hip-hop, so he could care less about the concert.

Texas Tech will play host to the first annual Red Raider Celebrity Tennis Tournament. The celebrity tournament will be very unique.

The political views on our dorm floor run the gauntlet from total anarchy to extreme fascism.

# Activity 3.10

In the following exercises, there are many AP Style errors. Correct all the mistakes you can find. Don't forget to look for mistakes in numbers, punctuation, capitalization and usage. Remember to use proper copyediting techniques.

1. After making monthly clinic visits to examine the supplement's effects on HIV transmission and on childhood mortality in the first 2 years of life, the researchers found that the mothers who had received vitamin A supplements during their pregnancies had a 42.4% transmission rate, while those that did not had a 33.8% transmission rate.

2. John Banzhaf, a GW law professor, is currently working on a case on behalf of Ashley Pelman and Jazlen Bradley, two overweight 8 year old girls that "we're lured into McDonald's with playgrounds and tiny toys," he said.

3. The class conducted legal research for the lawsuit and then passed it to a trial lawyer. Banzhaf said out of the 12.5 million dollars won in the settlement, 10 million dollars went to vegan, Muslim and Hindu organizations, and 2.5 million dollars went to lawyer fees.

4. The thefts occurred at 3995 Evergreen Pkwy. sometime between August 2-5. At least $40,000 of equipment disappeared.

5. Hotels and condominiums along Banyan Drive in Hilo experienced an extended power failure Sunday, according to a statement from Hawaii Electric Light Co.
An electrical short circuit in HELCO's underground power distribution system along Banyan Drive caused the failure, which began at 8:17 a.m. in the morning.
HELCO personnel transferred effected customers to alternate circuits and restored power from 9:29 a.m. to 12:57 p.m.

6. The group met Sun. at Eagle Point Park to decorate black t-shirts in preparation for its non-violent protest taking place at school today. The shirts areame to me with the idea of using this vehicle as a D.A.R.E. car for the Duncan Police Department," said Police Chief Ron Ward. "I approved, and we requested the District Attorney's office give us the vehicle for that use."
Ward said there is close cooperation between law enforcement agencies in Stephens County.

7. The group of students where what is known as Gothic-style clothing and believe certain students are being singled out based on clothing choices. Students also are protesting what they say to be Clinton high school principal William Cornelius's apparent refusal to meet with the group to discuss possible compromises.

8. The state has ordered McCready Memorial Hospital to reduce medical rates for the next three years, a state hospital official said, in order to repay patient overcharges and satisfy associated penalties.

9. By complying, the hospital's $1 million liability will be cut almost in half after a year, Maryland Health Service Cost Review Commission Executive Director Robert Murray said.

10. "Rates will be reduced until the overcharge is satisfied," Murray said. "(The hospital) was very cooperative in reaching the agreement."
Under the agreement, McCready will reduce patient rates by $217,000 annually for a total of $650,000 over 3 years, Murray said. Former patients won't be refunded for any overcharges.
The total reflects an estimated $450,000 in patient overcharges on a per case basis during fiscal year 2002 and $200,000 in associated penalties, he said.

11. Thanks to a dedicated Police Officer and a Chief who gave him the go-ahead, Duncan now has a DARE car for use in the fight against drugs.

12. A '93 Camaro Z28 was in the siezed property of the Stephens County District Attorney's Office. It had been taken from two people who were arrested and convicted of transporting drugs. Because the vehicle was used for the commission of a crime, Police were able to seize it.

13. For the 2nd year in a row, the University of Science and Arts of Oklahoma has been named the number one public, undergraduate college in the Western United States by U.S. News and World Report.

14. Released first on its website Friday, the magazine also calls USAO the "No. 1 Best Value" in the West among schools in the "Comprehensive-Bachelor's" category. The magazine's annual college guide was scheduled to hit news stands on Saturday.
Besides quality, USAO also earned praise for cultural diversity and for helping students achieve their educational goals with less debt.

15. The Almanac predicts that this year, the average temperature will be twenty-six degrees in Dec., 22 degrees in Jan., 14 degrees in Feb., then warming back up in March to an average temperature of 30 degrees. Weisser said those numbers may be realistic but may not be a far cry from what the numbers have been every year since the Almanac's first publication in 1792.

16. The Almanac, which hit the news stands Monday, contains weather predictions, planting tables and other helpful hints such as health tips, fashion trends and interesting feature stories; all enjoyed as Gospel truth by some and pure speculation by others.

17. For Region 10, which covers the Northern Great Plains and the Great Lakes, most of December and January will be mild with cold weather in late December and the first half of February.
Some people may say thats an obvious prediction.

24

18. The Lone Star State's best-known long, tall Texan has hit the half-century mark, and as much as we all love the State Fair of Texas' most recognizable symbol, how well do we really know Big Tex? Don't worry, this isn't an exposé about how the big boy with the big drawl likes to wear women's shoes and was originally made in Japan.

19. Turns out Big Tex is a real good ol' boy. Big Tex was born down in Kerens (near Corsicana) in 1949. He was a project organized by the Chamber of Commerce as a Christmas decoration. See, back then, Big Tex was a different icon -- Santa Claus. His fifty-two foot body was made of iron pipe from the oil fields -- can't get much more Texan than that, can you?

20. The Person Board of County Commissioners has already approved imposition of an additional ½ cent in local option sales tax. However, now that the North Carolina General Assembly has passed the enabling legislation statewide, the Person Commissioners will apparently have to do it again.

# Chapter 4
# Leads for Media Writing

## Introduction

No matter what kind of story you are writing, if the lead doesn't get the reader started into the story, the rest of your work is in vain. By working hard on beginning with something important, or capturing attention in some other way, you can ensure that the reader will continue in the story. Just be sure the lead is appropriate and accurate. You can get more practice in lead-writing by also completing the activities in Chapter 13.

## Key points

- Writers must capture the reader's attention immediately.

- The basic summary lead summarizes the story by putting the most important point in the story at the beginning.

- Leads are not wordy, usually.

-

- Narrative leads can be effective when there is a compelling narrative to follow.

- Descriptive leads work best when the writer uses excellent detail to show the reader a verbal picture.

- Don't overstuff a lead with all five Ws and one H. Usually some of those elements can wait.

- You should be aware of some of the classic lead problems and learn to avoid them, but remember the biggest problem of all is inaccuracy.

**Here is an important relevant website** where you can find more material on writing:

http://www.poynter.org/links

The Poynter Institute, a journalism school for professional journalists, lists more than 200 links that can help writers.

## Activity 4.1

Write a hard-news lead for the following information.

> Ralph Francona, 63, had a good day at Persimmon Hill Golf Course. He shot an even-par 72 and missed a hole-in-one by six inches (on the par-3 No. 15).
>
> The rest of the day, well, won't rank among his highlights.
> Alice Marie Francona, 59, wasn't having a good day. She'd missed out on a Tupperware party because her husband Ralph didn't get back from the golf course on time.
>
> Eyewitness Minnie Landis, 68, of 3417 Riverbend Drive #104 saw Ralph Francona arrive at the condominium complex in a disheveled condition. "He looked like he was plastered; I mean three sheets to the wind."
>
> Landis said the ensuing argument was over Francona's lateness and his condition. Landis saw through the open glass door at the rear of the #112 condo that Alice Francona pulled a club from Francona's golf bag and whacked him repeatedly over the head with it. Police said the club was a steel-shafted Taylor Made 8-iron.
>
> Francona suffered a minor concussion and cuts over his left eye that required 37 stitches, police said. Alice Marie Francona was arrested and charged with battery. Ralph Francona is retired. His wife works part-time at The Dollar Store, 350 Jersey Lane.

## Activity 4.2

Write a lead summarizing the most important facet of the poll.

Your news organization (newspaper or local magazine or TV newsroom) has just conducted a poll of 443 local residents by telephone from Monday to Saturday of last week.

The poll was concerned mostly with lifestyle preferences and media use. Your university's department of journalism sponsored the poll, which was supervised by 12 of its graduate students and professor Dwayne Nordby.

Sixty-eight percent of those polled said they were 'likely' or 'very likely' to spend a free afternoon or evening participating in active sports while only 42 percent said they were likely to spend a free afternoon or evening watching sports on television.

The most popular leisure activities are: socializing with friends (83%), dining at a restaurant (82.5%), reading a good book (75%) and working on a hobby (71%).

But the area isn't just for playtime. The poll found that 44.3% work more than 40 hours a week to earn a mean income of approximately $36,500.

The survey also seemed to indicate that the area remains a hotbed for high-technology jobs. Thirty-seven percent said their job was involved in some form of high-tech industry.

Fifty-three percent say they read a newspaper daily and 37 percent say they watch daily television news (though only 18 percent say they watch national news). Seventy percent subscribe to cable or some form of satellite TV and 65% own a personal computer.

# Activity 4.3

Write a lead based on the following information. You may also write a descriptive news feature lead as well.

Police Detective Evan Perez was out of uniform last month as he sat in court waiting to testify in another case. He was wearing a faded red shirt that had a round patch that said Alpine Fences and old black jeans tucked into Doc Maartens boots. He looked scruffy. He meant to look scruffy. Suddenly a man in a gray plaid shirt sat next to him.

"What are you in (here) for?" asked the newcomer.

"Cocaine. Had it in my pants," fibbed Perez, not wanting to reveal his identity.

"Me too. They found it in my car trunk. Say, you want to buy a couple of ounces?"

"Uh, sure."

So there in District Judge Robert Hernandez's courtroom and they surreptitiously set up a buy for yesterday. Today, Roland Vera, gray plaid shirt and all, was arraigned on charges of selling two ounces of cocaine.

Perez, a police detective for six years, still laughs about it. "I just kept thinking what gall this guy has to had to sit in court and talk about selling cocaine."

Perez has played a dope dealer for years but the courtroom performance was the toughest. "Throughout our conversation, I really expected a fellow officer to walk by and say, 'Hello, detective',"

Perez said. "I'll not forget this."

## Activity 4.4

Write a basic summary lead based on the following information:

Who: Lottery director Marcelo Vera

What: A press conference was held about the lottery's performance last year

Where: In your state capital

When: Yesterday, at 3 p.m.

What: "The lottery sold $805 million worth of tickets according to an audit of last year's sales. That amount ranks our state sixth nationally and first per capita of all states."

Why: "I think we had an excellent campaign explaining how our program benefits all of our students who choose to attend a public state university through the Lottery Scholarship Program."

How: The audit was conducted by the state's accounting office and compared with national figures.

# Activity 4.5

Here is some historical information about Old Head, a promontory in Ireland that was converted into what many consider one of the world's great golf courses. You may want to examine the course in more detail at www.oldheadgolflinks.com or to check historical facts on InfoTrac.

Scenically awesome and rugged, the Old Head is the only definite known place directly connected by historians and academics with the Eireann Celtic tribe. It is local assumption that the Eireann tribe gave their name to Ireland as a whole, Ivernia being a classical old name for the country. The Old Head remained the stronghold of the Eireann, but the Goidelic invasion broke the tribe and ended their period of influence.

Navigational Fires: Its importance remained, and in the Old Irish triads, it is named as one of the three old buildings in Ireland. Legend has it that the Eireann were the first to light a navigational fire (light) by their fort as a guide to fellow settlers who came in friendship. The headland is also closely associated with the Later Iron Age (200 BC to 400 AD), the first habitation by the Eireann which was continued by their conquerors. To this day, some enigmatic traces of human settlement remain on the Old Head, visible as small circles of stone which are likely to be the remains of huts from that Later Iron Age.

From the past - a shining light for the future: The modern Old Head of Kinsale lighthouse, completed in 1853, is situated at the southern extremity of the peninsula. However, the original Old Head navigational lights were by the site of the old castles. The ruins remaining stand as testimony to this site of the first Eireann navigational fires. Legend claims these were never allowed to go out. These lights remain part of history used as a warning signal in 1601 as the British forces of Kinsale awaited the 24-strong invading Spanish fleet of warships which was subsequently to be besieged in the harbour for 100 days before the famous Battle of Kinsale. Two of the most famous ship losses off the Old Head of Kinsale were the City of Chicago (1892) and the Lusitania (1915). This latter tragedy was instrumental in bringing the United States into World War I and thereby changing the course of history. There have been countless other wrecks in the vicinity of the Old Head over the centuries. Ecological Sanctuary: The Old Head Golf Links has been constructed with a defined and clear ecological tenet underlying all aspects of the development. The aim has not only been to preserve, but also to enhance the natural layout of the site, which has long been recognized as a prime Irish ecological haven. Hence the habitats of all the animal species off the headland will be retained and encouraged, and in addition, a flora planting program has been undertaken that has imported a spectrum of native maritime species from all five continents. This will ensure that the site retains its position within the "Inventory of Outstanding Landscapes in Ireland".

## Activity 4.6

From the following information, write a basic summary lead.

Who: Bishop Xavier Roman of the archdiocese of Harbinger.

Why: Selected because of a 23-year stint leading charity work for the state's underprivileged and other civic activities.

Where: The Founders' Day parade begins at the corner of Stovall Boulevard and Norsworthy Avenue and finishes in the City Square with speeches by the mayor and the parade marshal.

How: The Harbinger Chamber of Commerce annually selects the parade marshal.

What: Roman is the grand marshal for the 94th Founders' Day parade in Harbinger on the first of next month. All Harbinger schoolchildren are given the day off and a large celebration takes place downtown.

# Chapter 5
## Research for Media Writing

## Introduction

Researching helps find information that writers can include within a story, can use to craft interview questions, or can use to develop story ideas. However, the most important reason to research subjects is to avoid errors. Some common research tools include dictionaries, phone books and maps, but can also include Internet searches and electronic databases.

How much research is enough? As much as possible, given the restraints of time and availability. But you will find the restraints loosen when you gain confidence in approaching stories through research.

## Key points

- Research may begin with easy-to-use tools like dictionaries and phone books, but will probably also include trips to the morgue or the modern electronic library.

- Learning Internet research skills is vital, but remember to carefully evaluate information gleaned from cyberspace.

- Public records are extremely important sources for many public affairs stories.

- Press releases must be accurate since many reporters will take information from them for distribution to their audience.

- In an interview setting, a dumb question is one that you should have learned through basic research.

**And here are some important** relevant websites where you can find more material on research.

http://www.gao.gov
http://www.muckraker.org
http://www.inil.com/users/dguss/wgator.htm
http://www.nicar.org

NICAR is the National Institute for Computer-Assisted Reporting, a program of Investigative Reporters and Editors, Inc. and the University of Missouri School of Journalism.

http://www.ire.org/

IRE is the Investigative Reporters and Editors, associated with NICAR.

http://ww.iabc.org/links

IABC is the International Association of Business Communicators.

Using InfoTrac College Edition, you may enter the following terms for key word and subject searches: Free Speech, First Amendment, ethics in journalism within the following periodicals: American Journalism Review, Variety, Columbia Journalism Review.

## Activity 5.1

Use InfoTrac College Edition to double-check information in this story. At least one fact is wrong and an important fact is missing. Then use the information at the end of the story to write a descriptive lead.

AUSTIN, Texas -- The Rev. Jessie Jackson said President Lyndon Johnson's efforts in forwarding civil rights have been almost forgotten.

"There's no doubt that Johnson advanced the cause as much as anyone." Jackson said to a crowd of about 600 at a ceremony at the LBJ Library on the University of Texas at Austin campus.

"And he faced obstacles at every turn." In Johnson's four years as president, Jackson said, he cemented the civil rights actions that had begun under President John F. Kennedy. Jackson appeared courtesy of the LBJ School of Public Affairs. Jackson said that George Wallace's 1968 presidential candidacy came about because Johnson refused to bow to southern segregationists.

"I can only pray that Texas' newest president will not undo what this man has done," Jackson said in reference to George W. Bush.

Jackson also paid homage to the late Texas political figure Barbara Jordan, who taught classes in the LBJ school. The event took in the LBJ Library auditorium with some familiar faces in attendance. Notables included former Texas governor Ann Richards, former Texas senator Lloyd Benson and former President Jimmy Carter. Jackson was dressed in doctoral robes and, at one point, stood directly under a large blown-up photograph of Johnson and a much younger Jackson.

"Who is that young man?" Jackson quipped. The event honored Jackson for his role in civil rights legislation through the years.

## Activity 5.2

You will want to use InfoTrac College Edition to check information in the following story. There is at least one factual error that appears.

Murray Sperber blames it all on Blutarsky, Otter and the rest of the Deltas.

The Indiana University english professor said that the movie Animal House became the perfect compliment to big-time college atheletics in universities foregoing academics in favor of beer and circuses for their students. The phrase is an allusion to the bread and circus that Athenian emperors used to keep the citizenry happy.

Animal House popularized the concept of drinking one's way through school, said Sperber, who has authored a book with the title Beer and Circus. It's not uncommon for graduates to remember nothing that went on inside a class room, or so they tell us after they graduate.

This attitude, he says, goes hand and hand with the dominance of college atheletics on most campuses. Sperber, a critic of the NCAA who has drawn the ire of former Indiana basketball Coach Bobby Knight and his supporters, had to take a year off in Montreal when he received numerous death threats after Knight's firing.

So he has an idea or two about the state of college sports today. First, despite everything, Sperber remains a sports fan. But what has come to pass as sports on campus has become anything but fun.

Sports has become a big business and that business succeeds because it creates a need for circus-like entertainment. He discussed universities that blatantly violate the spirit of academics by passing atheletes who have no business in a classroom.

He said that's no surprise at NCAA trouble spots like SMU or Nevada-Las Vegas, but it even happens in Ivy League schools like Colgate.

Sperber said that popular culture has so ingrained the concept as university as circus that it will take a full and complete effort by faculties and university administrators to stem the tide and regain control of their classrooms.

## Activity 5.3

Write a summary news story based on the news release below. Be sure to look out for errors in numbers. You will want to decide which facts are important enough to print and which are not.


Survey Shows Confused Consumers Mistakenly Think They're Eating Right


HARBINGER – Most Americans may think they're eating right, but a recent survey shows that they aren't necessarily eating right.

A just-released Purcell & Associates survey of 1,000,000,000 primary grocery shoppers revealed some noteworthy discrepancies between what consumers believe about healthy foods and the stuff they actually consume, and the effect their eating habits have on their nutritional health.

For example, according to the survey, 83 percent, or six out of seven, of consumer respondents were aware that bread and other grain foods provide energy. More than 70 percent correctly agree whole and enriched grains can help prevent heart disease and cancer, and also can help with weight control.

"Americans understand benefits of consuming grains and other nutrient-rich foods," said Cheryl Liljestrand, M.A., R.D., author of Eating After Yet Another Diet Fails and consultant to several nutritional clinics. "We need to address ways to motivate consumers to put that information to use in their daily lives."

Despite knowing the health advantages of breads and other grains, Americans don't appear to have a clear idea of just how much grain foods they should eat. Americans believe, incorrectly, that they need to eat an average of 43 servings of bread and other grain foods each day.

That number is less than the actual amount of bread and other grain foods needed. The USDA Food Guide Pyramid, considered by most as a sensible and healthful eating plan, includes the recommendation that people consume an average of six to 11 servings of bread and other grain foods daily, depending on age, gender, and activity level.

When it comes to actual consumption, USDA data shows Americans are getting, on average, 6.8 servings of grain foods daily, barely meeting the minimum recommended serving, with women getting only 5.5 servings a day. USDA data also shows Americans aren't getting enough of the nutrients bread and other grain foods provide. Although more than four-fifths of consumers indicated they think they are getting enough fiber (78 percent) and complex carbohydrates (76 percent), in reality, only 55 percent are getting enough fiber and 52 percent are getting enough complex carbohydrates.

"With the glut of nutrition information and misinformation available to people, it's no surprise their beliefs and practices don't exactly match," said Liljestrand. "The average person is simply confused by all the conflicting health data available. Factor in the countless fad diets that have little nutritional basis but promise great results, and consumers' knowledge about healthy foods, such as breads and grains."

Dietitians also are concerned about Americans' eating habits. An independent survey of 390 registered dietitians showed 86 percent don't think consumers ages 12 to 45 are getting enough grain in their diets. Ironically, weight control and disease prevention, the health benefits consumers most commonly associated with bread and other grain foods, are among patients' top concerns, according to dietitians.

"It's good news that consumers recognize which foods are good for them and what those foods can do," said Sharon Rudd, president of the Wheat and Grains Cooperative Council. "We need to find ways to give consumers permission to get more grain foods into their diet so they can take advantage of all the benefits. A couple of pieces of enriched bread, rolls, whole-wheat bread, whole-grain crackers, or a plate of pasta each day can help prevent heart disease, cancer, birth defects, and more. It's just too bad most people don't know it."

The Wheat and Grains Cooperative Council, in cooperation with the Bakers Association, commissioned a survey by Purcell and Associates of the primary grocery shopper in 1,000 households. Respondents' households were randomly selected and telephone interviews were conducted from July 31 through August 26, 2002. The margin of sampling error associated with a sample of this size is plus or minus three percentage points at the 95 percent confidence level.

# Activity 5.4

Please write a story using the information below, but you will need to double-check the percentages and company spellings (the dollar figures are correct). The lead is provided for you in bold.

**A late surge in buying failed to alter the worst Christmas shopping season in 10 years, said analysts today.**

According to figures for same-store sales, the recession took a bite out of some of the nation's largest chains.

Traditional retailers felt the sting badly, analysts said. For example, J.C. Penny dropped from $2.3 billion to $2.29 billion, a decrease of 3 percent.

Sears and Rowbuck fell from $3.895 billion to $3.89 billion, also a decrease of 3 percent in same-store sales.

Carter Hawley Hale took the worst licking this season in same-store sales, dropping 3.7percent from $361 million to $355.7 million.

May Department Stores fell from $1.666 billion to $1.660 billion for a decrease of .7 percent.

However, some chains raked in the bucks, none more than so than the Gap, which jumped from approximately $270 million to $305 million for a 12 percent increase in same-stores sales. Analysts were pleased because the Gap not only held onto but increased its sales after a spate of new stores opened a couple of years ago.

Wal-Mart and Kmart did well this Christmas, with Wal-Mart increasing from $4.25 billion to $4.47 billion for a 10 percent increase. Kmart jumped from $4.40 billion to $4.45 billion for a 3 percent increase.

The stores recovered from a dismal November, normally a big sales season. Instead, analysts said, total sales actually dropped .1 percent.

The retail industry measures the percentage change in stores open more than a year because total sales may be skewed by new store openings, which tends to increase business for a brief period of time.

# Activity 5.5

Write a story from the following information. However, be very careful about the numbers given below - the percentages and totals may not be correct.

The Harbinger County Commission unveiled next year's budget at last night's meeting.

The biggest increase went to sheriff and fire services, hardly a surprise since three new commissioners emphasized those issues in last November's election. The budget, if approved, gives a 5 percent increase for sheriff and fire services, jumping from $6.1 million to $6.8 million.

The biggest percentage increase, though, went to county recycling which jumped 40 percent. Recycling director Vijay Khator was pleased to hear that the recycling program goes from $600,000 to $920,000.

"I can promise you that we can use all of that money," he said.

Taking the biggest hit was road construction, which declined 12 percent from $7.7 million to $6.8 million. Part of that cut, said commissioner Bill Nahorodny, came from the elimination of the deputy roads commissioner position. "It just doesn't make sense to fund a position now handled by the county works commissioner."

Still, county works also tumbled in the budget from $11.1 million to $101 million for a decrease of 7 percent.

The total budget increased 3 percent from $79 million to $94 million, said commissioner Dan Boyd.

# Chapter 6
## Interviewing Skills for Media Writers

### Introduction

Successful interviewing is important to your ability to find facts and support them with quotes. Some interviews are done for purposes of background information, while other interviews are meant to obtain quotes you can use in your story. Remember the acronym PHUFA (Prepare beforehand, Handle the interview, get Useful quotes, and pay attention to Fairness and Accuracy). As part of accuracy and fairness, it is important that the quotes you use be in the proper context. Tape recorders are usually more useful for magazine writers while time constraints make them less useful for many newspaper reporters. Tape recorders may well help your accuracy. Proper use of quotes includes understanding the basic use of quote marks, including quotes inside quotes, quotes with multiple paragraphs, partial quotes, and complete sentences inside quotes.

### Key points

- Preparation is important

- Remember who is in charge

- Remember your needs

- Be fair in your quote selection

- Be accurate in your reporting

**And here are some important relevant websites** where you can find more material on interviewing skills:
http://www.poynter.org

http://www.powerreporting.com
A resource for any number of subjects that an interviewer might face.

http://www.gate.net/~barbara/index.html
Barbara's News Researcher's Page can also be helpful.

http://www.ire.org

http://www.facsnet.org

http://www.jour.lsu.edu/perkins/InterviewingNalder.htm
Louisiana State instructor Jay Perkins has a great site that includes this interview with reporter Eric Nalder.

## Activity 6.1

One of the reporters on the police beat gives you an interesting tip. He's tied up on another story, but apparently a Wisconsin man was on the internet talking to a suicidal Boston woman last night. He helped police find her and save her. The woman is alive and in the hospital. If you can track down some more information, the story will make a good feature story for your newspaper, The Boston Globe.

The guy's number is 555-1435, but the reporter doesn't know the area code, just that the man, Jeffrey Ehrlanger, lives in Madison. You find the man's area code and call him.

Jeff: Hello.

You: Hello. I'm trying to reach a Mr. Jeffrey Ehrlanger.

Jeff: This is he.

You: Oh, good. My name is _____ , and I'm a reporter with The Boston Globe. Mr. Ehrlanger, you...

Jeff: Please, call me Jeff. I know Ehrlanger is kind of a mouthful.

You: Jeff, I heard that you helped a Boston woman last night.

Jeff: Yeah, on the internet. Is she okay?

You: Apparently she is still in the hospital, but I haven't verified that. Can you tell me a little about what happened?

Jeff: Yeah, I came home from work and just to unwind a little, you know, I got on the internet. I started talking to this lady. I saw her profile and it seemed like someone I might want to chat with. Just out of the blue, I started chatting with her privately. But then she was like all freaking out and saying she was going to commit suicide and stuff. You never know who you are talking to in those chat rooms, so I thought someone was just playing a bad joke. But then I started to think maybe it was true.

You: Where were you? I mean, what room were you in?

Jeff: It was a message board on America Online. That's where I usually go. I like it because I can meet interesting people or just find something cool to talk about or something.

You: So what exactly made you begin to think this whole thing was real?

41

Jeff: She was talking in too much detail. It seemed more than just random. She was saying that she was a dentist and wanted to be a dentist for kids someday. Then she just went downhill.

You: What do you mean?

Jeff: She said she was always feeling down, that she was manic-depressive had been hospitalized and everything. I asked her if she had ever tried to kill herself before and she said, "Oh, yeah. A bunch of times."

You: What happened next? How did you find out who she was?

Jeff: I got her to tell me her real first name, or at least I thought it was real. I couldn't be sure. Obviously, I knew here screen name, and she told me she was in Boston. It was hard, you know, wanting to find out real quick who she was and everything, but I didn't wanna spook her. I just tried to calm her down.

You: Did you know that she was trying to commit suicide as you were talking to her?

Jeff: Yeah. Then the next thing she told me was that she had cut herself and blood was going down her arms. I tried to get her to tell me her last name and she wouldn't. I asked her if she wanted help. She said no."

You: What did you do then?

Jeff: I started thinking, 'I need to call the police,' but I still thought maybe it was just some dumb kid goofin' off. But I didn't want the whole thing to be true and for her to die and for me not to have done nothing to help. So I finally make up my mind to call, and then I can't.

You: Why?

Jeff: Because I was on the internet. I only have one line in the apartment. When I realized it, it just made want to puke, I didn't know what to do. I was stuck between, do I keep talking to her, or do I leave and go to another phone and leave her hanging? I just thought about it for a second and thought, look, if she really wants to do this, she's not going to get online first. On the other hand, there was only so much I could do by talking to her. It was a huge risk."

You: But obviously you did call the police. Did you have a cell phone or something?

Jeff: No, I acted like I was chatting still, but I was running around the building like a maniac. I needed someone to call the police. I made a bunch of calls on the phone in the lobby that is downstairs. I finally got through to a person at the Madison police.
She said to call Boston 911.

You: What did they say?

Jeff: The operator said they couldn't do that much because I didn't have a last name or an address. What were they supposed to do call up every person named Sarah in Boston?

You: You did all of this downstairs in the lobby?

Jeff: Yeah, on the phone down there.

You: But what about Sarah? You obviously weren't responding to her.

Jeff: That's why she signed out. When I came back she just signed out really quick. Maybe she knew what was up.

You: How long had you been away?

Jeff: Five minutes. I thought that there had to be something they could do. With all the technology and everything. So I called back to the Boston police. This guy said that there was a federal law about this kind of stuff. In an emergency, the internet company can tell you their name and info and everything.

You: So they called AOL?

Jeff: No I did it. I called all around trying to get their number. I kept getting the number your computer dials into. Finally I got the right number and found a person and explained everything. She was the emergency operator. I gave them the screen name.

You: So what happened after the whole thing? When did you find out the outcome?

Jeff: When you called, I didn't even know if Sarah was alive or gone. I was hoping police would call me to tell me what happened, but I had no idea if I'd ever hear about it again. I'm obviously very, very glad that they were able to track her down and help her.

You: Well, thanks to you, right? It was quite a night for you. You've obviously calmed down a little since last night. How did you feel when you were going through all this?

Jeff: It was really unbelievable, and terrifying. I'm surprised that the whole thing worked out, especially when you think about all of the hoaxes everyone hears about and all the cyber-terrorism that is going on. Those hackers shut down a bunch of sites just last week. I love the Internet, but the problem is, there's no way of knowing what someone's emotion is. You have to kind of evaluate the whole situation in an instant and ask whether this is something you should act on or whether you should wait and see if the person is joking.

You: Can I just get a little more background on you? Your age, what you do?

Jeff: I'm 29 and I work with senior citizens in a center here at the university. I also live on campus, in an apartment. I used to play baseball in high school. I was pretty good. My dad played Triple-A.

You: Oh, wow. I used to play third base in high school, couldn't hit though. Jeff, can I just get you to spell your last name for me again.

Jeff: Sure, it's E-R-L-A-N-G-E-R

You: There's no "h" in there?


Jeff: Nope.


You: And you prefer "Jeff"?


Jeff: Yep. Jeff. Only my mother calls me Jeffrey.


After thanking Jeff and getting his work number in case you have any follow-up questions, you call the Boston police department and speak to Kevin Jones, the police spokesman. He tells you more about the woman. She lives in Boston in an apartment on Newbury Street in the Back Bay section of the city. She is 29. Police officers located her around 9:15 p.m. She had fresh cuts on her wrists and told police to get out, that she didn't want any help. Taken to Beth Israel Deaconess Medical Center and treated and examined. He won't reveal her name.


You also call AOL, but the spokesman says he was not aware of the incident.


You remember Erlanger talking about hackers, and you remember reading some stories on that in your paper. You check the archives and learn that cyber-terrorists forced some Web sites to shut down last week. They were a book-selling site, an online travel agency and a popular search engine. The search engine was only down for an hour, but the travel agency was down for the entire day. The online bookstore was down for a few hours.

## Activity 6.2

Write a news story from the following news release and interview (you may remember it from Chapter 2), but be careful, this is not a particularly well-written release in style and format.

WE ALL SCREAM FOR ICE CREAM! Jack and Diane's Ice Cream Shoppe will be the very proud sponsers of the first annual Harbinger Ice Cream Eating Championship.

There will be 3 divisions at the event: kids, teen-agers and adults. Jack and Diane's have decided to host the event at Harbinger Elms Mall Saturday at 12:00 noon on June 21, which is the longest day of the year, according to the calendar.

Anyone interested in participating in the contest should contact Jack and/or Diane at their shop at 3707 Jolliffe Avenue.

There is a form to fill out and a medical waiver to be signed by all competitors. Jack and Diane Bleske are co-owners of the popular ice cream eatery. All potential eaters will have 10 minutes to eat as much savory Jack and Diane's ice cream as they can.

The winner will be the one to completely finish the most containers of Uncle Gene's Vanilla Bean ice cream within the allotted time. Kids will compete by eating Gooey Purple Vanilla ice cream.

Jack and Diane's is the only locally owned ice cream to have placed in the Top 20 nationally in the prestigious Golden Scoop awards presented by the National Dessert Makers Association, which consists of restauranteurs and professional chefs who specialize in desserts.

The Bleskes have placed in the Top 20 for the last 4 years. Please call Diane Bleske at 555-9830 for more information.

You call Jack and Diane's Ice Cream Shoppe and talk with Diane Bleske.

"We read about this idea in the National Dipper magazine. It's designed for independent operators of ice cream stores around North America. We thought that it would be a good way to get more awareness of our product in the community."

"We are negotiating with the mall to see if we can lease some space in the food court. Right now, there's not actually a national tenant in there and we think we would be a great fit in that mall."

"Ice cream headaches? Yes, they can be a part of this experience. Some people think if they drink some ice water just before the event that that will ward off the headache. Others think a shot of tequila will already give them an antidote for the headache, but it happens sometimes when you eat anything cold in a hurry."

"We're obviously hoping for a big turnout. We've been doing some in-store advertising and sending out notices to our mailing list. Anyone who fills out a kids' birthday form with us is added to the mailing list. We don't sell that, but we do let people know about special events."

"We make 89 different flavors of ice cream, though we usually just stock about 40. We have some that are adult-oriented with liquor flavoring and others only a kid would actually eat, like the Gooey Purple Vanilla."

"Our vanilla has been among the best in the country and most ice cream connoisseurs use vanilla for tasting because of its purity. The idea is that you can't hide any imperfections in vanilla, the texture and the flavor have to be spot on."

"Let's see, Jack graduated with a degree in hotel and restaurant management from the University of Nevada in Las Vegas and I graduated with a degree in business management from Northern Arizona University. We've been married eight years. That's a lot of ice cream."

"Jack's favorite flavors are vanilla and Amaretto Ice. I like anything with chocolate chips and nuts in it."

# Activity 6.3

Write a story topped with a summary lead based on this statement from Harbinger police chief W.D. Espinosa:

"We are announcing today a new initiative for Harbinger drivers. We think it's a step toward improving safety on the highways and streets of Harbinger. Beginning next Monday, the Harbinger Police Department will begin the "Just Buckle It' campaign designed to increase seat belt usage among drivers in the Harbinger area.

"We have actively begun the campaign with our personnel in our patrol vehicles. Starting next Monday, officers have been instructed to actively ticket any driver who they witness not wearing seat belts. We are ticketing at a maximum of $100 per violation. If drivers are stopped for any other violation and are found not to be wearing seat belts, then we will write up a second citation as well.

"Safety experts agree that the safest thing any driver can do is buckle the seat belt. We have decided to proactively help enforce the existing seat belt laws and, we hope, save some lives in Harbinger because of this action.

"According to our files, we issued 304 seat-belt citations in the year 2000. Our goal is to issue that many in the next four weeks."

"Yes, there is a push from the federal government for local communities to implement this safety measure. It's a good idea. Anyone who has been out there on patrol knows the danger of driving without a seat belt. The statistics tell us that most accidents happen within three miles of one's home and that a good percentage of those would not have involved fatalities had the drivers been wearing seat belts."

# Chapter 7
# Reporting and Writing the Feature Story

## Introduction

Feature writing differs from news writing in several significant ways, frequently including less emphasis on timeliness, more emphasis on the entertainment value of the story, and the writer's confidence that the reader will read the story to its end. These differences have an impact on how feature writers find their facts and how they structure their stories, with much less emphasis on the inverted pyramid. Feature writers may work for newspapers, for magazines, or for on-line publications, and each medium has its particular demands. Freelancers quickly become aware of the competitive nature of their writing, and of its relatively low pay.

## Key points

- Some newspaper feature stories are tied to the news and called news features.

- Some newspaper feature stories are not tied to the news and are called independent features.

- Magazine features frequently display more of the writer's personal voice, while newspaper features frequently display the newspaper's institutional voice.

- Query letters are an important tool for freelance writers as they compete for the editor's attention.

- The many different kinds of feature stories include profiles, how-tos, health and science, environmental, personal essays and many more.

**There are many interesting websites** that use feature stories or report on publications that use them. Here are a few sites that will help you discover more about feature writing.

http://www.newspapers.com
http://www.slate.com
http://ajr.newslink.org
http://www.ajr.com
http://www.poynter.org
http://cnn.com

## Activity 7.1

Use the following information and write a basic summary lead from it.

Then, using the same information write a news feature lead from the information.

Cornell Bradford nearly lost his life in a hit-and-run accident two years ago.

Police later found the driver, a 20-year-old college student named Jonathan Schlichter, who served six months.

But Bradford is out of the hospital and being honored with four others at the local Chamber of Commerce's monthly meeting as Young Entrepreneurs of the Year.

Bradford, 17, and his mother Enya Bradford responded to help from the community with home-baked cookies. When people requested more cookies, they began a home-based cookie business that now has 47 outlets.

Cornell helps bake Cornell's Cookies and helps with the packaging.

Four others honored include Dinh Nguyen, 23, who owns a successful pet supply store; Victoria Ramos, 26, who runs La Calle Doce, a seafood restaurant on 12th Street; William Rutherford, 20, who has two sports memorabilia outlets in town, and Amy Lightfoot, 27, who owns a Native American-based boutique.

The meeting is at noon at the Downtown Club on the 18th floor of the Strohmeyer Building.

# Activity 7.2

Here is some historical information about Old Head, a promontory in Ireland that was converted into what many consider one of the world's great golf courses. You may want to examine the course in more detail at www.oldheadgolflinks.com.

Remember the feature lead you wrote using the following information in Activity 4.5? By using Info-Trak to flesh out some of the history mentioned below, by checking the website at and by adding quotes from Michael O'Connor and Steve Davis, write a feature story.

Scenically awesome and rugged, the Old Head is the only definite known place directly connected by historians and academics with the Eireann Celtic tribe. It is local assumption that the Eireann tribe gave their name to Ireland as a whole, Ivernia being a classical old name for the country. The Old Head remained the stronghold of the Eireann, but the Goidelic invasion broke the tribe and ended their period of influence.

Navigational Fires: Its importance remained, and in the Old Irish triads, it is named as one of the three old buildings in Ireland. Legend has it that the Eireann were the first to light a navigational fire (light) by their fort as a guide to fellow settlers who came in friendship. The headland is also closely associated with the Later Iron Age (200 BC to 400 AD), the first habitation by the Eireann which was continued by their conquerors. To this day, some enigmatic traces of human settlement remain on the Old Head, visible as small circles of stone which are likely to be the remains of huts from that Later Iron Age.

The De Courcy Family: Its power centre gone, Dun Cerma is scarcely mentioned in Irish annals for centuries until the 13th-century Anglo-Norman invasion which was to lead directly to the Old Head passing to the De Courcy family. The De Courcy chiefs occupied the castle until they lost power in the 16th Century and the ruins remain to this day. Also remaining are traces of the church and dwellings of the monks who lived there in medieval times and who, by tradition, kept the navigational fires burning.

From the past - a shining light for the future: The modern Old Head of Kinsale lighthouse, completed in 1853, is situated at the southern extremity of the peninsula. However, the original Old Head navigational lights were by the site of the old castles. The ruins remaining stand as testimony to this site of the first Eireann navigational fires. Legend claims these were never allowed to go out. These lights remain part of history used as a warning signal in 1601 as the British forces of Kinsale awaited the 24-strong invading Spanish fleet of warships which was subsequently to be besieged in the harbour for 100 days before the famous Battle of Kinsale. Two of the most famous ship losses off the Old Head of Kinsale were the City of Chicago (1892) and the Lusitania (1915). This latter tragedy was instrumental in bringing the United States into World War I and thereby changing the course of history. There have been countless other wrecks in the vicinity of the Old Head over the centuries. Ecological Sanctuary:

The Old Head Golf Links has been constructed with a defined and clear ecological tenet underlying all aspects of the development. The aim has not only been to preserve, but also to enhance the natural layout of the site, which has long been recognized as a prime Irish ecological haven. Hence the habitats of all the animal species off the headland will be retained and encouraged, and in addition, a flora planting program has been undertaken that has imported a spectrum of native maritime species from all five continents. This will ensure that the site retains its position within the "Inventory of Outstanding Landscapes in Ireland".

QUOTES

Michael O'Connor, summer tour guide, Killarney, Ireland: "There's no question that the golfers all want to visit Old Head. It has joined Lahinch and Ballybunion as the must-stops for just about every American and Japanese touring group. "I don't play golf, but I have walked the course and the views are spectacular. You'll occasionally see some hares out by the holes as well."

"Some of my tourists debate whether Old Head can be truly called a links course because it doesn't have the sand dunes like Ballybunion. Others say that the course is by the sea and looks like a links course, so that it must be a links course."

Steve Davis, WXKI radio host in Tampa, Fla., who takes a golfing group to Ireland every summer: "Every golfer should play Old Head at least once. It's one of the world's most breathtaking golf courses."

"Pebble Beach (in California) is spectacular but you can only see the ocean on certain holes. At Old Head, you can see the ocean from every one of the 18 holes." "We spend our days golfing and our evenings in the pubs on the trip. We play some of the best golf courses in Ireland, but every year the group's favorite always seems to be Old Head. I can't wait to go again."

## Activity 7.3

Use the information on author Joe Haldeman's website: http://home.earthlink.net/~haldeman/ to prepare a feature on him.

Note that you will have to decide what angle to take. Be sure to use InfoTrac College Edition for any background information that might seem appropriate such as science fiction literature or common hazards while bicycle riding.

## Activity 7.4

Explore InfoTrac College Edition's research capabilities by searching for information about a historical figure that you have only heard about. Use this information to write a 2 to 3-page feature story with the theme of Did You Know???

# Activity 7.5

Using the facts and quotes that follow, write a newspaper feature story. Your instructor has the original printed version of this story.

Notes:

Cats quit using the litter box for many reasons

House Soiling is the most common behavior problem reported by cat owners for cats being euthanized/abandoned House Soiling includes urinating, defecating and/or spraying outside the litter box

Finding out why a cat stops using the litter box takes time, perseverance, and investigative skills

It's a myth that mother cats teach their kittens to use litter. Kittens use clean, loose material for elimination at four weeks by themselves

Cats do not find feces distasteful or disgusting, as is sometimes assumed by people--to them it is a form of communication with other kitties

Could house soil because of a medical problem--veterinarian should give a physical exam and run lab tests to diagnose diseases that could cause house soiling

Diseases that cause house soiling are diabetes, hypothyroidism, feline lower urinary tract disease, cancer, neurological disease, intestinal parasites, constipation

Age-related diseases like arthritis or impaired cognitive function can also be a cause

Could be the location of the litter box--in a high traffic area, a dark area, a dank area or the smell (from either urine or cleaning with a harsh chemical)

One should have two litter boxes for one cat, three boxes for two cats, and clean them daily) cats don't like the smell of perfumed litter

Can even have a preference for course litter or fine litter, clumping or non-clumping

Cat could have been traumatized in the litter box-don't try to capture cat to give medications while in the litter box

Could just be marking their possessions/marking territorial boundaries/displaying sexual availability-they always do this by rubbing scent from cheek glands and paw glands-spray when there is a threat to their territory, or when new carpet and furniture (cat is trying to claim it)

Also spray because: the owner has been away too long, they don't like their food or amount of food available, or didn't get enough play time

The veterinarian can help--other suggestions: change type of litter, or box location

Feliway is a synthetic pheromone that inhibits cats from spraying on areas with Feliway
Some kitties require anti-anxiety medication to kick the habit

## Activity 7.6

Using the facts and quotes that follow, write a newspaper feature story. Your instructor has the original printed version of this story.

Notes for a story on the Forks of the Wabash Pioneer Festival

Forks of the Wabash Pioneer Festival-Huntington at Hiers Park-borders Briant and Taylor streets and Evergreen Rd

Admission is $2 for adults, $1 for students, free for ages 5 and under

Proceeds to benefit local charities and historic restoration projects

Parking is free.

Festival to highlight pioneer living up to the mid 1800s

Settlers demonstrate pioneering skills-spinning, wool, churning butter, sewing and cooking

Wigwams set up by Wooland Indians

Miami Indians, settlers and military men (in costume)

New to the festival this year- a farmers' market with merchants selling profuce, dried flowers, honey and sorghum

Craft booths and antique dealers in abundance

Opening firearm salute at 10 a.m. by 1st U.S. Light Artillery 1812-will also demonstrate military drill at noon and 4 p.m. Sat. and Sun. at 2 p.m. and 4 p.m.

"Young'ns fun area"-giant straw maze, a rope bridge, and a wooden merry-go-round

Varsity Singers of Huntington North High School to perform every hour from 1 to 4 p.m. Masque and Gavel Club of Huntington North High School to perform "Wait Til the Sun Shines, Nellie, or So Long Simon Snivelheart"-a melodrama about a man who discovers a gold mine which leads to disasters-every hour from 10 a.m. to 1 p.m. and 3-4 p.m. Sat. and 1-4 p.m. Sun.


Cream separating techniques at 11 a.m. and 3:30 p.m. Sat. and Sun.

Sheep shearing at 11 a.m. 10:30 a.m., 3 and 5 p.m. Sat.-10:30 a.m.,1, and 3:30 p.m. Sun.

Before festival starts for Sun.-Breakfast at 7 a.m. and worship service at 8 a.m.-worship service conducted by Markle Church of the Brethren

Interview with Rowena Richardson-chairman of encampment

Works as X-ray technologist at Orthopedics Northeast in Huntington

"We've been trying to re-create life through our cooking prior to 1840, pretty much."

She packs and prepares all the meals-stew, ham, cabbage, green beans, greens, apple pie, pumpkin pie

"We make our menu very similar to what was available at that time. Tomatoes are a no-no."

Tomatoes weren't eaten in Indiana until the late 1800s

"There is a difference in how clothing is depicted. The clothing needs to reflect the time period you're doing."

Costumes made from leather, wool, and buckskin

expects 50 camps of traders-deal in goods from fur to leather.

"I will actually move in Thursday morning and stay until Sunday. I take vacation time off for that."

5 or 6 traders will stay from Johnny Appleseed Festival. Traders from Georgia and Texas to stay for the Apple Festival of Kendallville on Oct. 5 and 6

"This is my 21st festival as chairman of the encampment. I make out the invitation list, and I make sure everyone gets set up in an orderly fashion."

Her husband and son are part of cannon demonstration of 1st U.S. Light Artillery-will participate in cannon demonstrations- Tim (husband) Elijah, 19, and Caleb, 13-have been involved in "pioneer life" since they were born. First got into "pioneer life" though a muzzle-loading club her husband belonged to.

"He's an outdoorsman and hunter. We've always enjoyed history."

## Activity 7.7

Using the facts and quotes that follow, write a newspaper feature story. Your instructor has the original printed version of this story.

Notes for 0 to 150 in four and a half football fields

Larry Loftin drives a 1968 Dodge Barracuda which takes 1.23 seconds to travel the first 60 feet.

Loftin has been drag racing for nearly 35 years.

Roswell Dragway opens Saturday, October 5 for the racing season.

Anyone can race any car until midnight on Saturday for ten dollars.

Three classes of racing take place on Sunday: street-car, non-electronics, and Top ET.

Only cars that travel a quarter mile in 10.99 seconds or faster can compete in the Top ET. Loftin will race in the Top ET.

His 1968 Barracuda is named "Dream Catcher", was named by his wife, and is owned by his partner, Al Corzine.

His wife, Cleo, set a national record in 1971 in c-stock racing.

Dream Catcher has a 529 cubic inch/440 engine. "That takes cubic dollars," says Loftin

Roswell Dragway is located near retired Walker AFB (72 Le May Road).

Roswell Dragway is New Mexico's only sanctioned IHRA approved drag strip.

IHRA is an acronym for the International Hot Rod Association.

Roswell Dragway's track is 60 feet wide and a quarter mile long.

From starting line to end the track is 470 feet.

Roswell Dragway has a 100 foot concrete launching pad and concrete guard rails.

The pits of Roswell Dragway are paved.

Loftin owns Big O Tires in Roswell.

Dream Catcher peaks at 152 mph.

Loftin has a 15 year old grandson named Justin Walther who owns and is renovating a 1968 Mustang. Roswell Dragway's website is roswelldragway.com and the phone number is 624-2167.

"I can outrun an F-15 for a quarter-mile, but after that, the F-15 would blow right by us!"

"The first 60 feet takes 1.23 seconds - that's when (the car) plants you in your seat. It's an amazing adrenaline rush," says Loftin. "There is no feeling like it; the brutality of the car and yet it's so smooth ... the feeling is hard to describe."

"It's man and machine - you literally have to become one with the car to maintain control," says Loftin

"It's a controlled, timed event," says Loftin. "We will always fight against street racing."

"It's become such a fantastic family sport," says Loftin. "There are as many women and children as there are men. Some of the best competitors are women - and they match their cars!"

Several of the Roswell Dragway competitors exhibit their cars to local schools. "We tell the kids that without reading, writing, math, and knowledge of computers it would be hard to participate in this sport," says Loftin. "That's why education is so important."

"Roswell needs activities for people," says Loftin. "It's good, clean, wholesome fun."

## Activity 7.8

Using the facts and quotes that follow, write a newspaper feature story. Your instructor has the original printed version of this story.

Notes for story and recipe on making crab burgers:

Alice Levold makes crab burgers when she needs to make something fast-uses canned crab, mayonnaise cheese, celery, green onion and green pepper, spreads the mixture on buns and puts them in the oven.

Suggests making the crab mix in advance to save time. Good if you don't know when guests will want to eat.

She also makes burgers at home to take to her sister's house in Seattle-broils them when she gets there.

"It's easy to get ready. It's something you can serve when they want is. When you're ready, you just pop it in the oven for a little bit."

She says they are "nice to serve if you know company's coming."

Levold: "They are so good!"

Makes 8 sandwiches, but could serve a different number of guests depending on how hungry they are.

She once served four clerics who ate all eight open-faced Crab Burgers.

Discovered the recipe in the Seattle Post-Intelligencer in 1956-it came from Gordon Clinton, the new mayor of Seattle then

She was just married when she first started making meals. She'd only cooked cake and fudge before that.

One of the first things she made was as a bride was peach ice cream meringue pie.

Levold: "I've given that recipe to about a million people."

Levold: "I was married when I was 23, and I've cooked ever since."

Takes casseroles to bridge club's gatherings and church potlucks


Goes to Packwood Assembly of God

Still gets the recipe out every time to cook, even for her lemon pie she makes about 18 times a year

Strict recipe follower-says that when people wonder why a recipe didn't turn out well, it's because they didn't follow the recipe exactly-that they tried to substitute one ingredient for another.

Crab Burgers

1 can (6 ounces) of crab meat (not imitation)

1/2 cup mayonnaise

1/2 cup celery, chopped

1/4 cup green onion, chopped

1/2 cup green pepper, chopped

1 cup grated cheese (she uses medium cheddar)

# Activity 7.9

Using the facts and quotes that follow, write a newspaper feature story. Your instructor has the original printed version of this story.

Notes for story on stroke victim

Donna Hildermann, had a stroke at 37-little more than a year ago-it was on both sides of her brain

Before the stroke, she was overweight and had a history of high blood pressure and high cholesterol

Hildeman didn't realize how serious these health problems were. Then she started to get headaches. At first she was diagnosed with migraines.

Stroke left her in a coma. When she came to, doctors quickly discovered she was close to blind and only able to move her head from side to side.

Released from hospital when there was no longer an immediate threat to her life, moved to a care center, which informed her family she was a hopeless case

Her family refused to accept the news.

Oscar Hildeman, her husband, and Joshua Hilderman, 11, decided to take care of her at home

But she since she couldn't even move her body from side to side it was even hard to get her to and from bed-she couldn't do anything for herself-so the family had to admit it was too much

Many facilities refused to take her. Some would, but didn't hold out much help.

Riverside Nursing and Rehabilitation agreed to take her in and put her in therapy.

Her parents (in Rochester) were glad to find a place for their daughter, and felt lucky to have found a staff who thought they could help.

Her husband agreed and he and Joshua moved to Centralia from Tacoma to be closer

They live in a 1$^{st}$ floor apartment close to Riverside and visit daily, and sometimes bring her to dinner in their apartment

The therapists at Riveside classified Hilderman's stroke as "very severe"

The team are Scott Duncan, doctor of physical therapy; Joselyn Eitemiller, speech therapist; and Veronica Skelton, occupational therapist.

They were determined to see her regain movement-led to her extraordinary physical improvement

Riverside's rehab. Coordinator, Eitemiller, is proud of the work the staff has done.

The day the story is going to be published is the last day of National Awareness Rehabilitation Celebration. Eitermiller notes the timeliness. The celebration lasts a week.

According to National Rehabilitation Awareness Foundation:

Designed to celebrate the victories people with disabilities have made through rehabilitation, to recognize rehabilitation professional, and bring attention to needs of people with disabilities.

Hildeman's therapist say she is fortunate to have a helpful and caring family. Her parents visit regularly.

Her sister and brother- Dolores Bryant of Centralia and Danny from Rochester-visit also

The family are helping with the therapy and are largely responsible for her improvement.

Hilderman almost gave up on herself. She wanted her movement to return more quickly but said "my body won't let it."

Hilderman: "It's been harder on Josh than anyone." She wants to recover "better and faster" for Joshua. She wants have an more active role in his life. That's why she has been trying harder.

Her husband: This has turned our lives upside down. Josh was always asking, 'Why can't mom come home?' but it's better than at first when he couldn't see her-a lot better."

## Activity 7.10

Using the facts and quotes that follow, write a newspaper feature story. Your instructor has the original printed version of this story.

Notes for story on Bear heaven

Boyds Bear Country's grand opening in Gettysburg, Penn. this weekend, Sept. 27-29

Opened earlier this month-it's a 120,000 square-foot barn/store-five story, gabled roof, red barn, constructed on 132 acres of farmland

First store, has 70,000 plush bears, rabbits, and other animals.

Only place to see the whole collection of Boyds Bears

1980s-Gary Lowenthal created Boyds Collection of plush bears. The bears are also posebale and jointed.

The name comes from Boyds, Maryland, where the Lowenthal family lived at the time.

Headquarters in McSherrystown, Penn.

15,000 retailers carry Boyds products. There other products include resin figurines, clothing for babies and a Boyds Bears Lionel train set.

Products given as gifts, used for home decorating and collecting.

Collectors have a club called the Friends of Boyds -the members are called F.o.B.s.-has 60,000 members, according to Boyds PR manager-Tara Houser

2,000 people attended the first F.o.B. convetion in Gettysburg last year-4 day convention

Mr. Rougeout Interview Notes-

Jean-Andre Rougeot, CEO of Boyds Collection Ltd

About Gary Lowenthal-

"He felt strongly that you could build a business around making bears for adults and collectors. He though bears were being sold to kids so why not to adults, too."

About having a barn:

"It's so Boyds." Everything has a country, down-home image.

"The company's motto is, 'We make you smile, we make you sigh.' Bizarre and fun, that's what we're about"

"Every bear has a name. We have naming sessions and people go wacko."

"All the furnishings were bought at flea markets. We went to dozens of flea markets from Virginia to Pennsylvania to find them."

"Boyds Bear Country is a one-of-a-kind entertainment and shopping destination-to say the least. We have people who have spent six hours in the store."

Expects more than 500,000 people to visit in first year. Already a destination for bus trips-Boyds retailers are organizing bus trips to Gettysburg

Only items not available at the store are special editions made for Friends of Boyds.

Some items are available only at Boyds Bear Company-"G. Anna Gottahaveit and Friends," a 'Bearstone' tribute to die-hard Boyds collectors, Union and Confederate soldier bears named Mason and Dixon (14 inches, dressed in authentic wool costumes designed by Carolann Scmittl, Civil Was period clothing expert)

Other items to test-market at store-resin garden statues of bears and books for children

Customers can talk to Boyds designers about the new designs at the Bear Maker's Workshop-3rd floor

Also a Make 'n Take Craft Center-3rd floor-customers can dress their own bears or a wreath

Rougeot: "We can accommodate 100 people an hour in this area."

But they have to make reservations

Also on 3rd floor-resin collections Bearstones and Dollstones, and a room for only Friends of Boyds to relax

Bears for four seasons and holidays-displayed accordingly

Winter-Bailey and Friends collection-dressed in colorful knit sweaters and scarves-Bailey in quilted velvet dress under a faux-fur trimmed velvet cape-the display has the bears playing and sledding on a snow-covered mountain.

Bailey is named for Mr. Lowentha's daughter. One is named after his son, Matthew, as well.

When the company started, Tina Lowenthal (Gary Lowenthal's wife) made the outfits and dressed the bears. Now it is all manufactured overseas and all the clothing is designed to fit the bears.

Store full of various animals in cabinets, drawers, crates, bins, baskets-a 1929 Model A produce truck with bears for fall

Lower level-

All-you-can-eat family restaurant w/ sit down dining, food courts w/ sandwiches, baked potatoes, soups, and sweets. Adjacent general store has Boyds-brand snacks and drinks

1$^{st}$ floor: walk-through musem-history of teddy bears (100$^{th}$ anniversary of teddy bears) and Mr. Lowenthal the "Head Bean Hisself"-when he was a child in Brooklyn, teacher with the Peace Corps. Working at Bloomingdales in New York City-also the earlier Boyds bears are displayed

Company's mission to also help children-in fall, Boyds donates 100 percent of its profits from the sale of a resin figure or plush bear to Starlight Children's Foundation. Starlight Children's Foundation-nonprofit-addresses needs of seriously ill children and their families through in-patient and outpatient programs and services.

Reached $1 million with its 3$^{rd}$, and newest figurine-Joy Angeltouch and Everychild . . . Cherish Small Miracles

$1 million to fund Starlight sites at hospitals-the sites are themed fantasy playrooms where children can escape from treatment

Sherwood Forest themed lobby scheduled to open today at Johns Hopkins Children's Hospital in Baltimore

Rougeot: We looked into finding a place where the money goes to kids. At Starligh, about 89 percent of the money goes to the kids."

Boyds to donate 50 mobile entertainment units with TV, VCR, and Nintendo 64-can be wir child's bedside.

# Chapter 8
# Research and Writing Skills for Opinion Writing

## Introduction

Opinion writers attempt to persuade others through their writing. Editorials, reviews and columns are three common types of opinion writing seen in today's media. But these forms require more than taking a stand on a question. Good opinion writers know that they are also reporters, who must research, verify facts and use interesting writing to attract readers. Opinion writers use a structure that gets to the point quickly, backs up the opinion with facts and then has a strong ending rather than an inverted-pyramid fadeout.

## Key Points

- Editorials are the opinion of the newspaper, broadcast station, magazine or website as an institution.

- A newspaper, magazine or new-media column is the opinion of the person writing the column and not necessarily the opinion of the publication.

- Reviews should criticize fairly (don't knock a country singer for not performing opera), not reveal endings and inform the reader.

- Good opinion writing requires research; editorial writers should consult reporters and double-check facts.

- Opinion writing structures should begin with an opinion, follow with factual support for the opinion and finish strong.

**And here are some important relevant websites** where you can find more material on structures in opinion writing:

http://www.ncew.org
This website is home of the National Conference of Editorial Writers

http://www.psu.edu/dept/comm/aope/aope.htm
This website is home of the Association of Opinion Page Editors.

http://www.slate.com
Slate Magazine has a long list of political columnists (and some others).

http://www.sportspages.com
Includes a lengthy international list of sports columnists.

## Activity 8.1

Write an editorial that focuses on the changes in current mass media. One way to do this is to look at what happened when other major technology changes occurred. Use InfoTrac College Edition as your information source to find about the Penny Press, the advent of radio, the advent of television and other important changes.

## Activity 8.2

The following is a collection of facts pulled from a newspaper editorial. Based on them, write an editorial or a public relations position paper that either supports the provision written by Senator King or supports the environmental groups in opposing the provision. Be sure to include facts in your editorial, but also be sure to make it clear that this is an opinion piece and that you actually make your opinion clear.

Late in the last legislative session, state Senator Jim King of Jacksonville added a provision to a bill designed to help restore the environment in the Florida Everglades.

The provision was a pet project for Sen. King, who is in line to become the next president of the state senate.

It is designed to keep citizens' groups from contesting the state government's development decisions. It states that for a group to have legal standing to challenge a permit granted by the state Department of Environmental Protection or one of the state's five water districts, it must have been incorporated in the state for one year and must have 25 members in the county where the project is situated.

Opponents say that it would be particularly difficult for environmental groups to fight destructive projects in counties dominated by a few industries, where local citizens may not want to publicly speak out in fear of losing their jobs or having their friends and families punished by these industries.

Recently, several groups from outside Manatee County challenged Florida Power & Light's plan to burn Orimulsion fuel at its Parrish plant in that county. They successfully argued that the tarry fuel would be a threat to both the air and water.

The state of Florida has been a focal point for the developer-environment controversy. The developers cite a demand for housing as the state's population has grown rapidly in the last 20 years. The environmentalists note that the Florida ecosystem is particularly fragile and the state's distinctive natural characteristics may be lost if developers "continue to pave over every last piece of property in the state." The Miami Herald columnist Carl Hiassen has built a successful career as a novelist by emphasizing the conflict in several of his fictional books.

The previous law allowed for an administrative board to hold hearings in such matters and that frivolous litigation was quickly dismissed. But not as quickly as the developers might want. If one builder is stymied by these groups, another may be able to build a similar project nearby and injure the first builder's business.

## Activity 8.3

Rent a video or DVD of a movie that was a major hit in theaters within the past six months. View the movie in one sitting, taking notes, and then write a 15-inch review of the movie. Be sure and include all the background facts that you can find through your research. Make your opinion clear. Compare your review to others in the class. Compare your review to others that you find in the media, using Info Trac College Edition to research those reviews.

## Activity 8.4

Write a personal opinion column about a single pressing issue in your area: traffic, crime, pollution of air or water, etc. Make sure your research is complete and turn in the research notes along with the column. Compare your opinion to those of others in the class.

# Activity 8.5

Below are interviews about an issue for the sports page or the editorial page. Write an opinion column choosing one side of the debate over whether to use aluminum bats in college baseball. In this exercise, you want to make sure that you also mention the arguments which disagree with yours, but then state why your opinion should be followed.

Facts:

College baseball, along with those who play in high school, Little League and youth baseball, started using aluminum bats in the 1970s.

The current bats are quite expensive, often costing $150 or more per bat, but these tend to last for a while. Wood bats tend to break often but run anywhere from $40 to $100 a bat.

Recently, some coaches have pushed for a composite bat. These are usually made from graphite and a variety of other substances, including Kevlar.

Over the years, the NCAA has begun to push for safer bats that have less power. The rate of home runs per game has dropped from 1.06 in 1988 to 0.80 last year.

The NCAA tests experimental bats based on the standard 34-ounce, 31-inch bat. It looks mostly for velocity off of the bat and tries to come closer to the way a baseball comes off of a wooden bat.

Here's what some folks have to say:

University of Harbinger coach Nelson North: "I'm a traditionalist and I wish we could play all of our games with wooden bats. But the economic reality is that only a few college baseball teams make enough money to use these. Metal and composite bats do cost a lot, but they are much cheaper than going through the wooden bats that a baseball team would go through in a season."

Retired Springfield Tech coach Bob Gamin: "I'm convinced that the ping of the aluminum bats keeps fans out of the stands and sportswriters out of the press box. I coached two years with those rotten metal bats and got out of the sport. It's just not baseball any more."

Harbinger Lutheran College coach Bryan Peters: "I pitched a little bit in college and I remember the sound of a line drive that missed my ear by about six inches. I did not even have time to twitch a finger. By the time I flinched, the ball was in center field."

Harbinger Lutheran College shortstop Mike Macaluso: "I played summer ball in a wooden bat league in Virginia. We played for 10 weeks and I cracked seven bats. My parents had to ship a $60 bat seven times. If they hadn't been able to afford that, I would have had to use a cracked bat or beg one. Another kid on our team got six of them from a buddy who plays for the Cardinals. The big leaguers don't have to worry about cost. The company gives them all they can afford."

Springfield News-Picayune sports writer Amanda Tomaini: "The solution seems obvious: Major League Baseball ought to subsidize college baseball teams by donating bats. The problem is that the major leagues will probably never go along with it. I mean, you're talking about millionaires who won't even throw more than a crumb to retired players from 50 years ago."

Retired major league catcher Allen Shirley, a Springfield resident: "The owners make enough money to make this happen. But they're too greedy for words. It's a shame, but the only way it will ever change is when some poor pitcher dies from a line drive off his skull."

Springfield Tech education major Karen Mayes, who is a fan of her college team: "I just think there's not enough wood for all of those wood bats. I like that the metal is environmentally better."

Harbinger Herald baseball beat writer Ray Glass: "With the aluminum bats, the college baseball game is like pinball. Yes, home runs are down, but not offense. It's really common to see a lot of double-figure scores like 18-12 and 22-19. That's football, not baseball. I know there are other factors but I think most of the credit or blame goes to those stinking aluminum bats."

University of Harbinger assistant athletic director Bob Howell: "With the newer bat standard by the NCAA, we will have bats that are pretty close to the way wood bats behave. And though I know that a well-struck ball still comes off the bat quickly, I would remind you that a well-struck ball can come off of a wooden bat pretty quickly as well. Herb Score was a star pitcher for Cleveland in the 1950s when he almost lost an eye when a line drive caught him in the face. It pretty much ended his career as a pitcher."

# Chapter 9
# Reporting and Writing for Broadcast

## Introduction

Writing for broadcast differs in significant ways from writing for print, starting with the idea that broadcast writing depends on the spoken word, not the written word. As a result, for instance, broadcast writers find that contractions are much more common but abbreviations are to be avoided. Broadcasters also must be aware of the short amount of time available to present their message. This time constraint, together with the transient nature of the broadcast media, means most stories are simple and very tightly constructed. The structure of newscasts have a major impact on how broadcast news is written, and "flow" is an important term to remember. The two most common techniques for structuring a newscast are blocking and counter-blocking. Both terms refer to the placement of stories.

## Key points

- Broadcast style differs from print.
- Broadcast writers have little time in which to present the news.
- Broadcast leads focus on immediacy.
- Keep it simple.
- Just "say" it.
- Be careful with numbers.
- Block or counter-block for newscasts.

**And here are some interesting sites on the Internet** where you can find out more information or see how broadcasters handle the news:

http://www.rtndf.org
(the Radio and Television News Directors Foundation. This is also a shared site for the RTNDA, or Radio and Television News Directors Association).

http://www.poynter.org
The Poynter Institute isn't just for print journalists. The school has a number of courses designed to help broadcast journalists.

## Activity 9.1

First, write a 20-second story outlining the new product launch and the problems. By the way, Twin Cities Chemical Company's corporate office is based in your station's market.

Second, analyze how this could be a more important story. Create an outline on the story and pitch it to your instructor (assignment editor/producer).

Twin Cities Announces New Product

Twin Cities Chemical Company's CEO Harvey Clewell II today announced that the company's new product Lessfat will be released this summer. Lessfat is an artificial product used to produce a spread similar to margarine and butter.

Your research shows that Twin Cities didn't develop Lessfat and is already being sued by the company that did create the artificial fat product (Bizzaro Chemical Company). Bizzaro is Twin Cities' primary competitor, with a product called Omphout. The lawsuit claims that Twin Cities used corporate clandestine activity to steal portions of the artificial fat's chemical formula.

The artificial fat product has an instant market in the dietary foods business because it has fewer than 10 percent of the calories found in animal and vegetable fat products.

# Activity 9.2

Write a broadcast story on Clewell's "resignation." You must decide how far to delve into the SEC investigation, remembering the information was received off-the-record.

Harvey Clewell II has been CEO of Twin Cities Chemical company for more than 15 years now. Yesterday evening, during a special meeting, the Board of Directors wound up in a turf fight with Clewell. This morning, your sources tell you that the CEO, apparently offended at his authority being placed in question, resigned.

You also learn that Board President Baird Wallace has temporarily assumed the role of CEO. This morning you learned that Clewell is apparently under investigation by the Securities and Exchange Commission (SEC) for improperly advising some potential investors about profit expectations at Twin Cities.

You call Wallace who tells you off-the-record that the investigation tipped the scale for the board and led to the fight at the board meeting and ultimately to Clewell's resignation.

Wallace has no problem with a news story that indicates that Clewell has resigned, but asks you that nothing be said about the SEC investigation. Since the investigation isn't public, you are concerned about dealing with the situation.

Your background file on Clewell says he's been with company since 1965 and was hired as a vice president in the general chemicals division. He had joined Twin Cities from Bizzaro Chemical Company where he been a Director of chemical plant operations (one step below vice president). He was promoted to Chief Operating Officer in 1970 at Twin Cities and was named CEO in 1976. Clewell has won numerous industry awards for contributions to management and volunteerism.

Twin Cities Chemicals had sales last year of $824 million. Its major products are used in a variety of ways and your company has patents on cleaning agents and other commercial/retail chemical products, carpeting fiber developments, pharmaceuticals and plastics.

You pull the information from the annual report that shows that profits had been $9.2 million in 1990.

## Activity 9.3a, 9.3b, 9.3c

Go back to the Activities in Chapter 2 where you rearranged paragraphs in order to practice print journalism structures. Using the information in those stories, write a 20-second and a 60-second broadcast news story for each of the three: the trial story, the emergency response story and the space story.

# Chapter 10
# Writing for the Web

## Introduction

Media writers certainly need to understand the special reporting and writing needs for writing for the Internet. But, they also need to know that good journalism is still good journalism, and the basics taught by classroom instructors and found in the text remain valuable tools for web writers.

The convergence of broadcast and print media is beginning now in several places around the country and the trend will certainly expand. While traditional media will continue to prosper, knowing how to meet the needs of a converged newsroom will be useful for future media writers.

## Key Points

- The basic skills for good reporting and writing remain important to Internet media writers.
- Learning HTML programming skills probably isn't necessary for most media writers.

- Tight, concise writing is important.

- Web writers need to be able to pull together elements of a story from broadcast and print sources.

- Web writers need to be able to link to other sites throughout a story.

And here are some places on the Internet where you can find out more about writing for the Web.

www.yahoo.com/writing_for_the_web/ has a number of good web-writing sites

www.msnbc.com has a number of blogs, including the exemplary Altercation by Eric Alterman.

## Activity 10.1

Find a news story in a newspaper or magazine that involves at least one well-known person and is of about 700 words in length. Retype the story on a computer in chunks of 100 words each to simulate one screen's worth of words.

Now go through and eliminate as many words as possible by linking to an image or graphic element that illustrates the phrase. For example, a story about Central High School would include a link to a photo of the school or the school's own website.

**Activity 10.2**

Take a look at this story published the front page of the regular print edition of the Harbinger Herald and ask yourself how the story might change to be presented on the Herald's website.

The Herald has a converged site with a local television station. What kind of video could be presented? What kind of audio? What kind of photographs? What kind of links might be included in the story's presentation? Should there be sidebars? What kind of material might be presented in those sidebars? The "hard landing" happened around 8:30 at night. How might the story change on the website as the hours went by?

Using the skills you've learned from reading Chapter 10, rewrite this story as a package for the web, assuming you need to have it online as soon as possible.

## Blazing Helpcopter lands safely on highway

- **A fourth-grade patient and crew members escape unharmed after the jolt on Highway 39.**

By WILLIAM ALBRITTON and JENNIFER LAWSON

A Harbinger Hospital Helpcopter carrying a 9-year-old girl began bellowing smoke over the Harbinger River Thursday evening and had to make an emergency landing near the village of Kilkenny in rural Harbinger County.

Neither the girl nor three crew members were injured when the Helpcopter landed with a jolt on the road about 6:30 p.m. on a relatively quiet county highway.

Crew members hurried from the helicopter and led the child away from the site. A second Helpcopter arrived about 15 minutes later and transported the girl and the crew members to St. Peter's Children's Hospital in downtown Harbinger.

"The thing was billowing smoke as it came down," said Andrea Buginsky, who was driving east toward a PTA meeting at Kilkenny Elementary School. She thought it was a crop duster at first.

Buginsky said crew members helped the child to safety as flames began to rise from the copter's tail section.

"We work very hard to be ready for these kinds of situations," said Karen Rosch, chief of public relations for Helpcopter. "We are in position to save lives every day. The girl wasn't hurt and the crew was fine. That's why work so hard at preparation."

The names of the girl and the crew members were not released by press time.

Rosch said the damaged Helpcopter was an hour into its trip, transporting the child from Springfield Community Hospital to Harbinger, when the warning lights began flashing.

Another witness saw a small ball of fire near the helicopter as it crossed over Kilkenny. One of his children said, "the helicopter . . . it's on fire!"

"You could see a long plume of smoke," said Dirk Lammers, of Boston, who was in Kilkenny at his sister's house.

He said it was headed toward Harbinger and then banked and landed. Lammers said he assumed it did not crash because there was no commotion.

"You have to give props to the pilot there. He has to be really sharp to get that down without a problem," Lammers said.

Buginsky, an engineer at Harbinger County Electric Company, said the pilot told her that dash lights flashed red and the Helpcopter began to smell of smoke and they knew they had to land.

"You can tell they have practiced for this," said Buginsky, 36.

After the girl and the crew members were picked up, a third helicopter retrieved the remaining crew member.

"All of them came in just fine; no problems to report," said Jessica Sims, St. Peter's Children's Hospital spokeswoman.

The Federal Aviation Administration will investigate why the twin-engine BK-117 was forced to make an emergency landing, said Eva Dworakowsky, FAA spokeswoman.

"I understand there may have been an engine fire," she said. "Were there mechanical problems? Operational problems?"

A Helpcopter maintenance crew dismantled the craft's rotor blades to make it easier to transport. The blue and yellow helicopter, its left engine and rear charred, was moved to a Springfield airport, home of their Helpcopter base, on a flatbed truck.

Rosch said the pilot and copter are from First Flight out of Bend, Ore. The company contracts out staff and equipment, he said.

Such pilots have to have at least 2,000 flight hours to do this kind of work, said Rosch, adding that representatives from First Flight will come to Springfield to check on the helicopter and the crew.

The Helpcopter folks will activate a reserve helicopter while the damage is being checked.

The last Helpcopter crash was on April 13, 1991, when the medical helicopter hit a radio tower near the Springfield River, killing all three crew members.

## Activity 10.3

On the Internet, find today's most important story on CNN.com site. Compare how CNN presents the story with how CBSnews.com, Foxnews.com, and NYTimes.com present the story. Looking at the ways in which the stories are presented (not at the content), in what ways are the presentations similar? In what ways are they different? Which story did you find the easiest to read? Which version offered you the most complete information?

How did your local newspaper's site handle the same story?

# Chapter 11
# Reporting and Writing for Public Relations

## Introduction

Public relations practitioners seek to effectively communicate with a number of audiences. Effective communication usually comes down to effective writing. When you examine some of the web sites below, you will notice that many of the links pages lead to sites about research, better writing, and news. Practitioners must especially learn the craft of meeting the needs of different audiences, internal and external. You should learn how to communicate effectively with those connected with your company or client as well as those outside of your company. Your messages should meet the needs of your audience, be it internal or external. Your newsletter should be understandable to the employees, your speeches should fit the occasion and the speaking ability of the presenter, and your news releases should meet the newsworthiness and deadline requirements of reporters.

## Key points

- The practitioner analyzes trends and public opinion, counsels executives, understands his or her institution or client, and can deliver effective messages to different audiences.

- The internal audience includes those connected with the company and is reached through company newsletters and magazines, brochures and annual reports.

- The external audience includes those publics outside of the company. These may be reached through news releases, backgrounders, position papers, speeches.

- A news release is not advertising or hyperbole. It relates newsworthy information to the media and other publics in a form that fulfills the public's needs.

- News releases should always include a contact person and his or her telephone number.

- Practitioners should understand media deadline requirements and ensure that releases are timed to fit within those deadlines.

**And here are some useful websites** for more information:
http://www.prsa.org (The Public Relations Society of America's site).
http://www.iabc.com (The International Association of Business Communicators' site)
http://www.prnewswire.com (This site that gives important financial news)
http://www.niri.org (National Investor Relations Institute's site)
http://www.newslink.org (This site offers numerous links to news organizations).

## Activity 11.1

This exercise is based on the Bob Evans Farms employee newsletter, The Homesteader. Rewrite into a story that informs employees about a new promotion. Be sure to avoid any hyperbole.

This offer is good only while supplies last. And this is a really stupendous offer. Guests at Bob Evans Farms restaurants will receive a Bob Evans phone card if they spend enough money on gift certificates.

The phone card promotion will be promoted on table cards, a counter place mat at the register and gift certificate posters featuring information concerning the phone cards. Employees in each of the restaurant's regions are eligible to win gift certificate prizes if they record the highest percentage increase in gift certificate sales.

This contest begins Nov. 19.

Only employees who work from Nov. 21-Dec. 25 during this year are eligible for the prizes. The phone cards are good for 15 minutes of talk time from Ameritech. Restaurant managers and hosts/hostesses from the restaurant in each region that sells the most certificates overall will also win gift certificate prizes. Really, really great gift certificates, too.

To receive a phone card, a guest must spend $25 on gift certificates.

# Activity 11.2

You are writing a news release for Eckerd Drugs as a public relations practitioner. Use a summary lead and a block structure to write this release for general release.

What: The Eckerd Corporation of Clearwater, Florida

When: next Monday

What: Three new vice-presidents at Eckerd Corporation
Who: Mona Furlott, age 42; Kurt Bruder, age 39; Joe Miller, age 46.

The vice president of express photo operations takes on the responsibilities of the operation of Eckerd's one-hour photo labs. That job is now Ms. Furlott's. She joined Eckerd in 1974 and has held a variety of positions with increasing responsibilities including Regional Business Manager, Senior District Manager and Area Manager. Her most recent position was Director of Photo Operations. She attended Saint Petersburg Junior College.

The vice president of general merchandise takes on the responsibilities of the merchandising activities for the categories of housewares, toys, stationery, electronics and seasonal goods. Mr. Bruder will serve in that capacity. Mr. Bruder joined Eckerd in 1984 and has held a variety of positions with increasing responsibilities including Category Manager, Senior Buyer, Buyer and Assistant Buyer. His most recent position was Director of Seasonal and Imports. Mr. Bruder is a graduate of the University of Florida with a Bachelor of Science degree in Business.

Joe Miller has become Senior Director of Photo Merchandising and will be responsible for all photo merchandise including film, cameras, frames, albums and overnight and one-hour photo business. Mr. Miller joined Eckerd in 1996 as Category Manager of Photo. Prior to joining Eckerd, he was a Category Manager with Revco Drugs and Hooks SupeRxDrugs. Mr. Miller is a graduate of Ball State University with a Bachelor of Science degree in Business

These appointments enhance the photo operations, general merchandise and photo merchandise businesses within our company and position them well for the future.

"Mona's 27 years of photo operations experience and excellent leadership skills will position us well for 2001 and beyond," stated Mr. Robert Aston, Senior Vice President of Operations. "She will continue to be an important contributor to our Express Photo Operations team."

Mr. Bruder and Mr. Miller will report to Enzo Cerra, Senior Vice President of Merchandising and Marketing.

"Kurt and Joe have both been and will continue to be important contributors to our merchandising and marketing team," commented Mr. Cerra. "Their combined merchandising experience of over 40 years will position us well as we move forward."

Eckerd Corporation, a wholly owned subsidiary of JCPenney Co., is headquartered in Clearwater, Florida and is one of America's largest retail drug chains with over 2,650 drug stores in 20 states including 140 Genovese locations, 1,350 Eckerd Express one-hour photo labs in 18 states and three pharmacy mail service facilities in three states. Eckerd Corporation's 2000 revenue was $13.1 billion.

Eckerd Corporation employs more than 78,000 associates company-wide including more than 8,000 pharmacists. Eckerd Corporation is one of the top five retail supporters of the Children's Miracle Network benefiting over 170 CMN-affiliated children's hospitals nationwide, assisting 14 million children annually.

(For additional company information visit our Web site on the Internet at or the JCPenney Web site at http://www.jcpenney.com.)

# Activity 11.3

Write a news release based on the following information. Be sure to use inverted pyramid as your structure. Write the release as if you were a public relations practitioner for the Americans for Consumer Education and Competition.

Now, part 2 is to use the same information to write a news release as if you were a public information officer for the school district that houses Woodrow Wilson High School.

Where: Washington, D.C.

Who: Woodrow Wilson High School seniors in the Academy of Finance

What: Will host a presentation of the "report card" of an exam about personal finance. Former congresswoman Susan Molinari, current national chairperson for Americans for Consumer Education and Competition, will preside.

Why: Scored twice the national average on a test of personal money management issues over high school seniors across the country. The test measured how much future leaders understood about personal finances and preparing for their financial futures.

"ACEC is proud of Wilson High students who took our exam and scored double the national average," says former Congresswoman Susan Molinari, currently national chairperson for Americans for Consumer Education and Competition. "Unfortunately, this is the exception and not the rule."

Who conducted the poll: The Tarrance Group & Lake Snell Perry & Associates

What else: Molinari then plans to conduct an informal quiz of the student audience on survey questions of particular relevance to teen-agers embarking on serious financial responsibilities. "If you save your hard-earned money to buy a car, then you should know how to get the best finance deal possible," says Molinari. "Parents need to talk about personal finances with their children and the wealthiest nation in the world should provide education on this critical subject in its schools."

Why: Incorporating financial literacy into school curricula is a main objective of ACEC and a provision in HR 61, a bill introduced in the U.S. House of Representatives that would provide funds to states to teach financial literacy skills and create a national clearinghouse of instructional information to assist in raising the level of financial literacy in America.

Who: Congressional Representatives David Dreier (CA) and Earl Pomeroy (ND), chief sponsors of the bill, will hold a briefing at the U.S. Capitol in HC-7 on Thursday, March 15th at 11:30 a.m. following the press conference at Wilson High.

What: "America's Money Skills Report Card shows us there is a problem and now we need to address it," says Molinari. "We owe it to our children to give them the tools they need to learn financial accountability. Teaching personal financial management in high school can help our young people avoid the pitfalls of debt and instead, make the smart choices when life's big decisions come their way."

# Activity 11.4

Write a lead for a general news release for the following event as if you were a public relations practitioner for APCH. Then recast the release as if you were writing the release for the APCH Newsletter. You will need different leads.

What: Starry Starry Night 2001: Celebrate the Children. The event is a benefit for A Place Called Home (APCH), a nonprofit youth center in South Central Los Angeles.

Who: CIBC Oppenheimer, an investment management firm is underwriting the cost of the production, assuring that all the evening's proceeds will go to assist the children and families of APCH.

What: For more information about Starry Starry Night: Celebrate the Children, or to buy tickets, contact the event coordinator -- Levy, Pazanti & Associates at (310) 555-5033. To learn more about APCH, call Debrah Constance or Ray Gallegos, APCH's Executive Director, at (323) 555-7653. Please also see APCH's website at http://www.APCH.org

Who: Starry Starry Night's cast of luminaries includes Jason Alexander, David Brenner, Julie Brown, Jasmine Guy, Monica Guy, Lea Thompson, Jo Beth Williams and some surprise guests. The evening of music and comedy, conceived and directed by Alexander, will include dancers and rappers from APCH's popular Creative Expressions program.

What: The gala will honor Richard Wiseley, Managing Director of CIBC and a member of APCH's Board of Directors.

Why: Last year, when Jason Alexander offered to produce and direct Starry Starry Night, the center's Board wasn't sure whether they could afford to accept his generosity. The quality show Alexander proposed would be costly to produce.

What: "We are so grateful to Richard and CIBC," said Debrah Constance, CEO and founder of A Place Called Home. "Our mission is to enable inner-city youth -- to help them find their dreams and lead a more self-reliant life," she said. "CIBC's generosity means that we can devote many more dollars toward those goals."

# Activity 11.5

Here's a public relations news release with its lead sentence intact. Remembering to emphasize the public relations aspects of the story, place the remaining sentences in order.

For Immediate Release
Transplant Procedure Performed at Harbinger Lutheran Hospital by Iadorola, Ensch and Associates and University of Harbinger Surgeons

HARBINGER, Aug. 27 /PRNewswire/ -- Ed Rocha, a 46-year-old Waxahachie, Texas resident, became the nation's second hand transplant recipient following a 13-hour procedure, Aug. 21-22.

The surgical team was led by Thomas E. Tucker, M.D., Iadorola, Ensch and Associates and assistant clinical professor of surgery at the University of Harbinger. Twila D. Blossom, M.D., assistant professor of surgery at the University of Harbinger, is managing the immunosuppressive therapy for both hand transplant patients.

An orthotist and hand therapist will begin bracing and hand therapy within the next few days. Rocha will be hospitalized at Harbinger Lutheran Hospital for the next two weeks and then will remain in the Harbinger area for three months.

"We anticipate a good result," Tucker added. "However, as with any operation of this complexity and investigative nature, the outcome cannot be predicted at this time. We will have a better idea of the long-term outcome in three to six months."

The news conference will be up-linked live via satellite and available for down link at coordinates Ku-Band SBS 14, Transponder 3, Vertical Frequency 13101 MHZ, 56 degrees West. The signal will be available from 4-5 p.m., Friday Aug. 28.

A special news conference will be held at 4 p.m. (EST), Friday, Aug. 28, to announce the completion of the landmark operation. The conference is scheduled in the Harbinger Lutheran Hospital Friedlander Heart and Lung Conference Center, 11th floor, 8913 Bova Blvd.

After surgery, Rocha was placed on a combination of immunosuppressive drugs at a reduced dosage to lower the risks associated with the anti-rejection medication. Those risks include a higher incidence of cancer, infections and other disorders. "Mr. Rocha is under observation for signs of rejection and will have biopsies every four days. We will also monitor his progress with other lab tests and evaluations," said Dr. Blossom.

The group of surgeons performing the experimental procedure also performed the nation's first single hand transplant on Robert Saito two years ago. Harbinger-Springfield Organ Donor Partners, an organ procurement organization, coordinated the donation of the hands for both.

A partnership of physicians and researchers at Harbinger Lutheran Hospital, Iadorola, Ensch and Associates Hand Care Center, PLLC, and the University of Harbinger developed the pioneering procedure. A hand transplant, unlike solid organ transplants, requires multiple tissues (skin, muscle, tendon, bone, cartilage, fat, nerves and blood vessels) and is called composite tissue allotransplantation.

In 1999 Rocha, a bookkeeper and father of six, underwent amputation of his non-dominant left hand at the wrist as a result of a fireworks accident involving a three-inch mortar. Prior to the transplant he used a cable hook prosthesis.

The procedure, which began at approximately 8 p.m. (EST) Friday, Aug. 28, involved an 18-member hand surgical team and five-member Anesthesiology Associates team. The recipient is listed in stable condition at Harbinger Lutheran Hospital, based in the Harbinger Medical Corridor.

"The reconstruction on this patient went extremely well," Dr. Tucker said. "We encountered no unanticipated problems. The reconstruction was difficult at times because of the extent of damage to the patient's muscle as a result of his initial injury."

Complete press packets including b-roll and still photography of the surgeons and patient will be available to the media at the briefing. Information, photography and streaming video are also available on our web site.

# Activity 11.6

Using the facts listed below, write a news release from the Springfield Cancer Center announcing the 15<sup>th</sup> annual FACTors conference and its guest speaker Sara Julieta. The following are facts that can be used in the release.

Who:  FACTors (Fight Against Cancer Together) group at Springfield Cancer Center and Research Institute and the American Cancer Society

What:  15<sup>th</sup> annual FACTors conference and "New Beginnings" workshop

When:  Saturday, October 5 from 8 a.m. until 3:15 p.m.

Where: The Highclass Suites Hotel, 3705 Main Blvd., Springfield

An update on the advances in the fight against breast cancer will be by Richard Cox, M.D. He is the founder and mentor of FACTors. He is the program leader for Springfield's Comprehensive Breast Cancer Program.

Featured workshops will cover a variety of breast cancer related topics such as updates in detection and treatment of breast cancer; advances in breast reconstruction; an interactive yoga workshop; and a presentation of Integrative Nutritional Therapies, a book by Dr. David Johansen. The keynote speaker is State Representative Sara Julieta (D-Springfield), a breast cancer survivor.

The conference is open to the public. Reservations are recommended since there is limited space. Call 1-555-5555 for reservations or information.

There is a $25 fee for registration and it includes breakfast, lunch, and workshop materials.

FACTors is a network of breast cancer patients that provides information, support and a sharing of experiences for persons diagnosed with breast cancer.

Sara Julieta, formerly treated at Springfield Cancer Center, said, "Adequate funding for research, early detection and quality treatment for all will save the lives of 3000 women a year in our state. This is my hope."

The "ask the experts" panel discussion will be moderated by Bay News 12 Business Editor Tara Gafney.

## Activity 11.7

From the facts listed below write a news release from the Springfield Zoo. You may want to interview a classmate or your instructor, who could pretend to be a zoo spokesperson.

Springfield Zoo is one of the world's largest zoos. It features 2,700 animals representing 320 species.

Two Eastern white-bearded gnus, also known as wildebeests, were born this week at Springfield Zoo.

The wildebeest calves and their mothers are doing well and appear healthy as they graze the northern portion of the zoo's world-renowned wildlife refuge area.

The calves, now 40 pounds may reach 400 pounds when mature.

These animals are commonly found in Kenya and Tanzania on Africa's east-central coast.

# Activity 11.8

Organize the following facts in a press release from Raymond James Financial geared towards an external audience. The purpose of this release is to promote their charitable contributions through the "Kicking for Kids" program with Tampa Bay Buccaneers place kicker Martin Gramatica.

About the program

The 2002-2003 football season marks the third annual season for the "Kicking for Kids" program.

Raymond James donates $500 per field goal successfully completed by Martin Gramatica and $250 when there are no completed field goals.

The contributions go to a children's hospital located in the city where the game was played.

Since the program began two years ago, $28,750 has been raised for children's hospitals around the country.

Hospitals that will receive contributions from the program this year include St. Petersburg's All Children's Hospital, Tampa Children's Hospital at St. Joseph's, Arnold Palmer Hospital for Children and Women in Orlando, Detroit Medical Center's Children's Hospital, Cincinnati Children's Hospital Medical Center, Children's Memorial Hospital in Chicago, The Children's Hospital at Carolinas Medical Center, Johns Hopkins Children's Center in Baltimore, Children's Healthcare of Atlanta, Temple University Health Sciences Center in Philadelphia and the Children's Hospital in New Orleans.

## About Martin Gramatica

In the 2001-2002 football season, Martin Gramatica kicked 23 field goals.

Gramatica was the place kicker for the NFC Pro-Bowl team in 2000.

## About Raymond James Financial

Thomas A. James is Raymond James Financial Chairman and CEO.

Raymond James Financial's asset management subsidiaries currently manage in excess of $17.5 billion.

Raymond James Financial (NYSE-RJF) provides financial services to individuals, corporations and municipalities through its three investment firms, Raymond James and Associates, Raymond James Financial Services and Raymond James Ltd.

Raymond James Financial has 5,000 financial advisors in more than 2,100 locations worldwide.

## Quotes

James said, "We are very pleased to support Martin in this program, his work on behalf of children is very much appreciated in communities throughout the country."

James said, " It is a true pleasure to be a part of such an extraordinary program with a phenomenal person like Martin who is willing to reach out and help those in need."

Gramatica said, "I am proud to be associated with Raymond James in this program, and I believe that those of us who are fortunate enough to have our health have a responsibility to support the research facilities and hospitals dedicated to the care of children so more kids will be able to lead healthy lives."

## Activity 11.9

Using the facts listed below, write a summary lead and the first paragraph for a press release. Remember, not all facts belong in the first paragraph.

In 2001-2002, the United Ways across the nation raised an estimated $5 billion.

Monies raised goes to assist with critical issues in America's communities.

Last year, corporate giving to all philanthropy declined by 12 percent, but corporate giving to United Way remained constant.

Last year, $4.7 billion was raised.

The resources raised in 2001-2002 include the annual campaign at $3.95 billion.

Planned giving and outright endowment gifts are $83 million.

In-kind donations are $267 million.

Leveraged community resources are at $235 million.

The September 11 fund is at $501 million.

The number of people who donate more than $500 to United Way has increased.

Brian A. Gallagher, President and CEO of United Way of America said, " We believe that United Ways performance in fundraising is a vote of confidence from our donors for the impact we are making in the nations communities."

United Way programs do more than fundraise and allocate funds, it brings together communities to set agendas that focus on the communities' most pressing issues, build coalitions to help advance these agendas, increase investment in these agendas, and measure, communicate and learn from the impact of their efforts.

# Chapter 12
# Research and Writing for Advertising Copywriting

## Introduction

The skills that make good reporters and public relations practitioners apply to good advertisers: the ability to write persuasively and tightly, the ability to quickly research a subject, the willingness to revise a piece until it improves. Though advertisers employ creativity, they learn to harness that creativity to meet the client's needs. And though an advertiser may be a wizard at video, print or web design, the substance of the ad outweighs the format.

## Key points

- Advertising isn't just random creativity, but the harnessing of creative ideas to specific goals that are related to customer needs.

- Copywriters must learn how to write to varied audiences and to respect those audiences instead of underestimating them.

- Copywriters would do well to remember Ogilvy's advice on producing advertisements that stay on target.

- Being able to produce a persuasive message means being able to give that message in as few words as possible.

- Copywriters seek to match motivations to reach customers.

- The purpose of an advertising campaign is not to produce really slick ads, but to sell. And to do so without lying.

**Here are a pair of useful websites** for more information on advertising and advertising copywriting.

http://www.aaaa.org (The site of the American Association of Advertising Agencies)

http://www.aaf.org (the site of the American Advertising Federation)

# Activity 12.1

Idea Generation and the Paper Clip

"Brainstorming" is the traditional method by which copywriters come up with the longest possible list of ideas. Here quantity is more important than quality because you never know when a dumb idea will trigger the next brilliant one. Only when you're tapped out of ideas, do you go back and look for the good stuff.

Your goal with this exercise is to practice some brainstorming.

You'll need a paper clip -- or a pile of them -- for inspiration.

Imagine you're advertising the unappreciated paper clip. How can you make people look anew at this lowly but dependable product.

1. List at least 50 ways people use -- or could use -- paper clips. Try not to edit yourself. No idea is too trivial or ridiculous at this stage.

2. Next, look at your list of 50 and identify a short list of your most unusual ideas.

3. Now, focusing on unusual uses for paper clips, write 25 headlines that "reposition" the paper clip as an old product with many uses. (Remember, Arm & Hammer Baking Soda isn't just for baking anymore.)

## Activity 12.2

Product Features, Consumer Benefits and a Used Car Ad

     In copywriting, "sell the sizzle, not the steak." In other words, advertising should sell consumer benefits, not product features. In this exercise you will learn to convert product features into consumer benefits.

     Imagine you're selling your own car in a classified ad. It's time to write 100 words of your car's benefits to potential buyers.

     1. Generate a list of all your car's features. Don't forget to include those "customized" options you added to the car, like the $1.54 in loose change down in the seats.

     2. Convert each one of your car's features into a benefit to its next owner. (Example: a lighted visor mirror is a feature, but the ability to check your teeth for spinach before a date is a benefit.)

     3. OK, you're ready to write that 100-word ad emphasizing the benefits of owning your old car. You're paying by the word so be concise. On the other hand a little drama or narrative makes for interesting reading, and that's important, too. Don't forget a "call to action": "Call 000-000 today for a test drive."

## Activity 12.3

From Abstract to Concrete

In advertising, memory and recall are crucial. If people don't remember your message, you've wasted your time and money. Funny thing about our brains, we tend to remember concrete images better than abstract ideas. Ad copy that helps people paint a mental picture is more memorable and so, effective.

- Concretes are things we can see, hear, smell, touch, taste.
- Abstracts tend to fall into the category of vague ideas.

In any event, stick with the concretes so readers can make mental pictures to help them remember your product. In this exercise, you will -- you guessed it -- turn abstracts into concretes.

Writing either headlines or one-sentence body copy, turn the following into consumer benefits using concretes to evoke strong imagery:

1. durable pantyhose
2. shiny hair gel
3. fast tax software
4. loud stereo speakers
6. sporty car
7. nutritious cereal
8. fun nightclub
9. fruity drink
10. attractive watch

## Activity 12.4

Twisting Clichés

Word play is a staple of "breakthrough" advertising competing in a "cluttered" media environment. The goal of word play is to get people's attention. Be careful, though. Don't sacrifice the product in the name of witty copy.

Some common forms of word play include the oxymoron (sad joke), double entendre verbal (laughing matters) and chiasmus (work to live, not live to work).

Twisting clichés also can be effective in advertising. They surprise and entertain while you communicate the product message. Volkswagen twisted the cliché "Think big" with its "Think small" campaign. Successfully reminding people of the Volkswagen brand since the 1960s, "Think small" has become one of advertising's most famous twisted clichés.

Yes, yes, you've already learned to avoid clichés like the plague.

Good writers are supposed come up with powerful new metaphors. But in advertising, a good twisted cliché can suck in readers like a vacuum.

Your goal with this exercise is to experiment with twisting clichés.

1. Choose a product -- any product. If you need inspiration, scrounge around in your kitchen or medicine cabinet.

2. Develop a list of your product's consumer benefits.

3. Write down all the clichés you can think of even remotely associated with your product and its benefits. (Example: If your product were snack cakes, you might write "have your cake and eat it, too," "let them eat cake," "cakewalk," "a piece of cake," "icing on the cake," "pat-a-cake," "baker's dozen," etc.)

4. Now sell your product and its benefits by twisting a few clichés from your list. Try replacing one word or swapping the words' order.

# Activity 12.5

A Case of Research

You have been assigned to write the ad copy for two in a series of books concerning the mass media. These books are similar to the sort that Time-Life offer - popular histories that touch upon the major aspects in a particular field. Your company has decided to push two of the books - the history of advertising and the early years of television - as its test cases.

You should use Info Trac College Edition as your research tool to write a two-page letter to be mailed to your marketing base. The letter should describe the series, focus on the specialized areas and use specific interesting examples that you have gleaned from your research.

Remember that the purpose of the letter is to sell the books.

# Chapter 13
# Editing and Revision for Media Writers

## Introduction

Editing and revising are an important part of the writing process. Though the way you edit differs from medium to medium, in each case you will be expected to edit your own stories carefully and also expected to work with editors to improve your stories. One technique for self-editing is to get TRICI, that is, Take time, Read your story aloud to yourself, Isolate each line of your story, Change your context to help you see the story with fresh eyes, and Isolate each paragraph of your story to help improve its logic and flow. Freelance writers find it especially important to be able to edit and revise their own stories.

## Key points

- Get TRICI.

- Develop good editor/writer relationships.

- Clean copy is important.

- Edit for grammar and style, but also for larger issues like logic and flow.

- Learn from your editing mistakes and don't repeat them.

**Here are some websites** that may provide helpful information:

http://www.copydesk.org  (The website of the American Copy Editors Society.)

http://www.theslot.com  (This website features the wisdom of copy editor Bill Walsh.)

http://www.poynter.org

## Activity 13.1

Please write a summary lead and an inverted pyramid story from the following information. You may not want to use all of the information here. Then write a brief news release as if you were the public relations counsel for the Mercy Lutheran Church.

A man was crushed to death today.

Allen is survived by his wife Wilma, and five children, Guy, 15, Barry 13, Regina 11, Lester 8, and Mona 6.

When electricity to the hydraulic lifter was severed, the lifter shut down on the spot and the load of bricks fell on Kristopher Jerome Allen, 31, of 426 Garrison Avenue.

Funeral arrangements are not complete at this moment.

Allen was unloading bricks for the construction of a church and a power lifter failed.

The accident occurred when Donald Dimmitt, 48, of 8903 Happy Trails Drive, pulled the electrical cord on the power lifter. Co-workers thought, or so they say, he thought the device was not begin used. It was.

He died instantly, Coroner Terry Linkin said. Jack Stubblefield, 23, of 143 Petty Street, apt. 7, said that he was operating the lifter at the time and others agreed. He tried to warn Allen, but the victim could not move out of the way in time, the workers nodded.

"Some people just ain't careful on construction sites," Stubblefield, a strapping, 6-foot-2 well-tanned blond, said. "This is a tragedy that could have been avoided. Chris didn't have to die."

The accident happened at a lot on the corner of 78th Avenue and Bannockburn Drive. The Mercy Lutheran Church, pastured by Randall Haedge, bought the property earlier this year and plans to move in by December.

## Activity 13.2

Write a basic obituary based on the following information. Decide which facts are most important and place them higher in the story. Not every fact is necessarily needed.

Who: William J. "Sagebrush Jim" Culpepper, born Feb. 18, 1927, died yesterday.

What: Mr. Culpepper was best known as a country-music singer, Sagebrush Jim Culpepper. He fronted a band known as The Tumbleweeds.

Where: He died in Scottsdale, Arizona of natural causes.

When: Mr. Culpepper was a member of the Arizona Music Hall of Fame, the Screen Actors Guild and Veterans of Foreign Wars. He attended the First Methodist Church of Scottsdale.

What: Mr. Culpepper enlisted in the U.S. Navy on his 18th birthday and was in the Pacific theater at the end of World War II as a seaman. He worked as a handyman on several Arizona ranches and briefly worked in radio sales for a station in Gallup, New Mexico. He began a career as a nightclub - or, more correctly, honky-tonk singer - in 1950.

What: Near his end of his performing career, Mr. Culpepper moved to Branson, Missouri, where he sang live in several theaters.

How: Mr. Culpepper was considered a major regional star in the Southwest United States and he did a somewhat noteworthy national reputation. His biggest hit, "Cactus in the Moonlight," climbed to No. 8 nationally in 1972. He was also known for writing and singing, "You're Just Gila Monster Mean," a No. 20 charter in 1977.

What: The funeral service will be held at the First Methodist Church in Scottsdale at 10 a.m. Saturday with burial to follow at El Monte Cemetery.

Who: He was married three times to the late Edna Schilte, to Joy Lynn Platt of Nashville Tennessee and to Anna Beatrice Johansson, 40, who survives him. Other survivors include three sons, Charles Schilte, of Starke, Florida; Jimmy Platt of Nashville and Marshall Platt of Lexington, Kentucky; a daughter, Rebecca Platt Embree of Milledgeville, Georgia; and 7 grandsons and granddaughters.

WHAT: "Sagebrush Jim was a talented singer, about as good as you got in those days," said current singer Joe McManus. "I remember listening to him as a kid and I got to meet him a couple of times up in Branson. He never acted like a star, though, and was very humble about it all."

## Activity 13.3

You are working for a magazine that caters to college students. The Star Wars movie The Phantom Menace, which is called a "prequel" to the trilogy, will open on May 19. Tickets go on sale today, but for days people have been waiting in long lines. Your editor wants you to write a short feature about how the opening is affecting college life. He thought of the idea when he heard from an old friend whose son is waiting in line. You get the son's cell-phone number. The piece will run next week, but before the opening.

On May 12, you interview Andy Denny, a sophomore at the University of Texas at Austin, who was in line when you spoke to him on his cell phone.

"I got in line yesterday at 7 p.m., and they give out tickets at 6:30 tonight. I'm really excited. I've heard about this movie a few years ago, and I've been waiting ever since. I'm not done with exams, but I figured I'd come up here anyway. I was worried that I wouldn't be able to go, but my chemistry exam was yesterday and my poli. sci. exam is tomorrow, so I was lucky. The line goes all the way around the theater."

Also on May 12, you go to the Uptown Theater in Washington, D.C., where you find some college students waiting in line. You interview Jamie Davis, a student at George Washington University Law School in Washington, D.C., who was waiting in line outside the Uptown Theater in Washington.

"My friends were coming up to get in line yesterday, but I couldn't because I had to take an exam. As soon as it was over today, I came up here and waited with them. It was the next day. Otherwise I would have been here yesterday. By the time I got up here, the line was a block long, but that's okay because later the line was over two blocks long."

You also interview Virginia Hein, a sociology student at Georgetown University, who is waiting at the Uptown Theater.

"I've been waiting in line about 20 minutes, but I'm getting kinda hungry, so I might go grab a burger and head home. N.Y.P.D. Blue will be on tonight. I didn't have any exams because I took the semester off. Star Wars is okay. My boyfriend wanted to see it, and he said to get tickets if I could. But I'll just tell him the line was too long."

You remember hearing about a professor at the University of Florida who teaches a course about Star Wars. You track him down. His name is Andrew Gordon.

"Yeah, I'm an English professor here at U.F. For years, I've used the Star Wars movies in a class on science fiction. I'm excited about seeing the new movie, but I'm not going to camp out to see it. That's kids' stuff. I'm going to wait until the lines die down, maybe in June."

## Activity 13.4

Write a soft lead (narrative) based on this information. You might choose to write the lead from the perspective of Patti, Ann, or the police.

Patti Duplantis faced a problem that most parents face in the child's first couple of years of childbirth - how to get a child to sleep. She learned one trick - 15-month-old Annie seemed to drop asleep in minutes after being placed in her car seat and being taken for a ride.

Patti, age 20, took Annie Duplantis for a drive last night and then went inside a convenience store because she was thirsty. The clerk noticed that her 1989 Ford Taurus was leaving the parking lot. Patti's first thought was: "My daughter. He's stealing a car with my baby in it." As the man driving the car drove the Taurus down State Road 542, a sheriff's deputy tried to stop it for speeding, then heard a radio alert about the theft, Sgt. Kerry O'Connor said.

The suspect, who was released hours earlier from the Harbinger County jail, is David Milton Parry, 32, address unknown. He wouldn't stop and a chase of 55 mph in 35-mph speed zones ensued for two miles. Parry finally stopped the car on Padget Street, jumped out and ran north through a junkyard, O'Connor said.

The baby was found unharmed. According to police, Parry said he never even knew it was back there.

"I don't even think she woke up," one deputy said. "She's fine, just a little tired since she didn't get to bed until 2:30."

Parry was charged with kidnapping, grand theft auto, aggravated fleeing and eluding and resisting arrest without violence. He is being held without bond.

## Activity 13.5

You stare at the notes you jotted down at today's assignment. One of university's broadcast professors won a big-time award and you were there.

You show your notes to your editor, "We need a story on this. You will need to get more background on Murrow and to double-check the information about him that you do have. You can use InfoTrac College Edition to gain some perspective on this famous broadcaster."

YOUR NOTES (somewhat translated)

The Edward R. Murro (???) Award

Presented by Dr. Alex Tan, director of the Edward R. Murro School of Communication, Washington State University in Pullman, Washington. Tan: Thank everybody for coming. The Murro Award is given to one national broadcasting professor who has best shown a commitment to improving the standards of broadcast journalism education and broadcast journalism. A committee of professionals and educators carefully weighed our finalists this year and we are very proud to announce that Dr. Rhonda Walls is this year's recipient. Dr. Walls has taught here for 12 years. Her doctorate is from Syracuse University. Her master's is from Texas Tech University and her B.A. is from Southern Illinois at Edwardsville. She worked as a reporter and weekend anchor for 15 years at four stations. She teaches classes in broadcast news writing, media management and public affairs reporting.

About HERE you now realize are some interesting and complex doodles. You apparently missed some of the speech and -- well, you have only sketchy, undecipherable notes until...

As my daughter Cheryl told me on our way to high school this morning, "Isn't Murro some sort of TV god?" Well, maybe not exactly, but he's way up at the top of the mountain, I told her.

I think everyone in broadcasting should have romantic ideas about Murro broadcasting on ABC radio from war-ravaged London. And how Murro practically invented television newscasts. And how Murro had the guts to take on Senator McCarthy (Eugene???) when almost no one

108

else would. It doesn't get any better than that.

To get an award like this can be only described as marvelous. I will always be thankful to Dr. Than and the committee for the honor. The plaque will hang in my office as a reminder of how important a job we have in preparing future journalists. The $3,000 check will help pay for Cheryl's tuition. I thank my colleagues who provide me with inspiration and help at just the right times. And most importantly, I thank my students, without whom no recognition is possible. I reached an epiphany in my fourth year of teaching when I realized that I like students and I liked making a difference in their lives. They have given me much over the years and for that, I remain thankful.

## Activity 13.6

You have just been told to edit the following story for tomorrow's paper. You have 15 minutes. Get started. Your instructor has the correct version.

by Antigone Barton
Palm Beach Post Staff Writer

Just when you may have thought its not safe to go in the water again . . . its about as safe as it ever was, according to shark experts.

Those who study salt water predators say the only feeding frenzy they're worried about are the media kind, after a shark bit a 10 year old boy on Sunday off Jensen beach.

Corey Brooks of Port St. Lucie was swimming with friends about thirty yards off shore when a shark toar an approximately eight-inch gash in his leg. He was taken to St. Mary's medical center in West Palm beach for surgery that included more than onehundred stitches, according to witnesses. He was in satisfying condition on Monday; according to a hospital spokeswoman. Corey was one of about 38 million to 40 million people to get wet off Florida this year, but just one of about twenty-five to have an encounter with a shark, according to Marine Biologist Sam Gruber.

Which doesn't reflect a growing problem, Gruber said Monday.

"Some people will be bit this year just as they are every year," said he.

But that's far from the biggest danger that will face beach-goers this year, pointed out the University of Miami Rosenstiel School of Marine and Atmospheric Sciences' Gruber.

Of the approximately 78,000 incidents that will call for lifeguard's attention nationwide this year – including: drownings, near-drownings, speedboat accidents, and "being hit by a meteor," only thirty will be the result of encounters with sharks, Gruber said.

"A shark attack is the least you will have to worry about," he added, your going to have to worry more about getting run over by a guy riding a dune buggy on the sand."

If anything has changed in Fla waters, it's the number of people swimming there, concurred director of the International Shark Attack File at the University of Florida George Burgess. The shark population has not signifficantly increased, he said.

From the Treasure coast to Palm Beach county, lifeguards agreed with the experts on Monday.

And the day after lifeguards ordered swimmers out of the water after Sunday's incident, crowds were out in full force again at Jensen Beach, life guard Eric Tillman said.

"I haven't had one question about sharks," Tillman said. "Most people are oblivious."
(Copyright 2002 Palm Beach Newspapers, Inc.  Reprinted with permission .)

## Activity 13.7

You have just been told to edit the following story for tomorrow's paper. You have 15 minutes. Get started. Your instructor has the correct version.


By Lawrence Ulrich

Ensuring they won't abandon that profittable truck segment to General Motors Corporation when Ford stops building its mammoth Excursion in about 2004, Ford Motor Company has a new super-sized sport-utility vehicle in the works.
The auto maker is developping an extended version of the already sizeable Ford Expedition S-U-V, company execs said.

About a foot longer than courent Expeditions, the new modell will be smaller than the Excursion but closely match the size of the rival Chevrolet Suburban and Gmc Yukon XL, and should reach showrooms around 2005 or 2006. Company executives said Ford have ruled out only one thing. It will not built a Lincoln luxury version of the new jumbo sport-utility, despite GM's plan to sell it's 2003 Cadillac Escalade ESV by January. GM is billing the Suburban-based ESV as the worlds largest luxury sport-utility.

The plus sized Expedition will still be smaller then the Excursion, whose record-breaking size and thirst for fuel made it public enemies Number 1 for some environmental groups.

It will also be lighter and more fuel-efficient than the excursion, whose porky curb weight of nearly 7,200 pounds topps all sport-utilities.

Ford hope the Expedition-based truck's more modern chassis and sofisticated suspension will make it a tougher competittor for the Suburban, which outsells the Excursion by more than four- two-one.

"It will be less of a beast than the Excursion, more refined and spot-on for the market," said a Ford source.

Jim Hall, vice-president of consulting firm AutoPacific in Mich, said Ford overeached in trying to unseat the Suburban. "Ford's mistake was assuming bigger was better, he said. "The Excursion ended up defining how big was too big for an SUV."

Excursion sales fell thirty-two per cent last year to 34,710 trucks.

Environmentalists had no problem defining the Excursion as a symbol of sport-ute overkill. Before the Excursion's 1999 introduction, the Sierra club ran a contest to choose a nickname for the truck. The winner? The Ford Valdez, after the Exxon oil tanker that wreeked environmental havoc in Ala.

But the new model won't have to worry about being the poster boy for overgrown sport-utes. It will roughly mimic the Suburban's exterior proportions, but top it on interior space, Officials said.

## Activity 13.8

You have just been told to edit the following story for tomorrow's paper. You have 15 minutes. Get started. Your instructor has the correct version.

by Ilene Olson

CHEYENNE -- 30 blue paper angels fluttered, one-at-a-time, to the floor of the Herschler building artrium on Tuesday -- visual representations of children in Wyoming who have died of child abuse since 1990.

The event, a candle light vigil to remember those victims of child abuse, was a solemn one. It is held annually in Apr. to commemorate child abuse prevention month. Holding a paper angel, third- and fourth-graders from St. Mary's School silently lined the third-floor gallery above the buildings atrium.

In the atrium two floors below, Merit Thomas of the Wyoming Department of Family Services read the names of each of the victims, ranging in age from seven weeks to nine years.

"Stephanie, 10 weeks _ Tyler, 13 months ... Brandy, 5 years _ Adam, 7 years _ Baby girl, 7 weeks _ "

Last on the list was Braydien Paul Cox, 3 months, whom died at the hands of his father this last July in Evanston.

As Thomas read each name, one third- or forth-grader released an angel, fluttered and twirled two stories down to the atrium floor.

The visualization was effectiv.

Ashley Sainz, a 9th-grader at Carey Junior High, said, "seeing all of those coming down really made you think. It kind of hurt you inside."

Sainz was a member of Carey's combined choir that performed for the vigil. As child abuse victims' names were read choir members turned on battery powered "candles" in their memory.

At the conclusion of the program, the only sounds breaking the silence were occasional sniffles from the choir.

Wyo. state treasurer Cynthia Lummis said she served as guardian ad litem for abused children several years ago.

She represented a girl who had been sexually assaulted by her father, children who were raising their parents, and children who were suffering abuse from their parents.

"I saw a slice of life I didn't know existed in Cheyenne and Laramie county, said Lummis.

Rose Kor, director of Prevent Child Abuse Wyoming, said 1,493 documented cases of child-abuse occurred in Wyoming last year.

"That's the number of kids they know suffered child abuse of some form," she said.

Including unreported cases, national studies shows the actual number is probably two or three times greater, Kor said.

Lummis said victims of child abuse and children at risk must be identified. Which can be accomplished with the help of people who are willing to get involved, she said.

Some ninth grade choir members suggested ways to get involved:

Jade Grant said families facing problems about child abuse need to get into counseling.

Michelle Garcia said, "If you can see something is starting to happen, watch his kids for them for a while."

Jamie Johnson said the vigil made her more aware of the problem of child abuse.

"I thought it was good we were involved," she said.

Nicki Johnson said, "I think it's just kind of shows that something as sad as this can be good," she said. "We're all here to spredd awareness."

## Activity 13.9

You have just been told to edit the following story for tomorrow's paper. You have 15 minutes. Get started. Your instructor has the correct version.

By Tamara Lytle
Sentinel Bureau Chief

WASHINGTON, D.C. -- Money is one worry Florida Gov. Jeb Bush won't have as they campaign for reelection this coming fall.

And if Tampa lawyer Bill McBride finaly nails down the democratic gubernatorial primary -- the most expensive in state history -- cash is expected to flow their way as well.

Both political parties are determinned to spend whatever it takes to put it's man in the governors mansion.

Political analists say Bush has un-ending sources of money as both the governor of a high-profile state and the President's younger brother. Democrats hope that the momentum that pushed MacBride neck-and-neck with Janet Reno in tuesdays election will draw major contributions from Unions and party members throughout the country.

"When your name is Bush you don't have any trouble raising money nationally, do you?" said Samantha Sanchez of the non-profit National Institute on Money in State Politics. If the race gets close, he'll raise alot more. The republican party is not going to let Jeb Bush loose for lack of money. He has a good phone number in his pockets."

President Bush is expected to return to Florida for yet another fundraiser with his brother, an Administration source says.

Democratic national committee spokesman Bill Buck said the president has selfish reasons, as well as familial ones, for doing everything they can to re-elect his brother.

"Florida is the most critical state" in the next presidential campaign, Buck said, so electing Jeb Bush is "the highest priority of the president's re-election strategy."

Karl Koch, a Tampa Democratic strategist, said Democrats now has "wind in their sails" and will do everything they can to get McBride elected.

## Activity 13.10

You have just been told to edit the following news release. You have 15 minutes. Get started. Your instructor has the correct version.

Microsoft, Yahoo! And America Online Support

Blood Donation Awareness Campaign

Wash., D.C. September 5, 2002 – The american red cross today launched a month long Togeether, We Can Save a Life public awareness campaign with the support of microsoft, Yahoo!, and America online. The campaign will educate americans about the importance of giving blood which has a limited shelf-life, on a regular basis and for a lifetime. With the help from these leading technology company's, the american red cross is leveraging the power of the internet to increase blood donations and ensure a safe and stable blood supply in support of our Nation's public health and security.

Blood shortages – especially during the Summer and Winter holidays – are chronic in this country. A continuous supply of blood will only be assured for those in need if enough persons regularly donate blood. American's can now learn more about the crucial need for blood donations and how to schedule appointments through online features (such as http://blood.givelife.org and aol keyword: Gift of Life), links and PSAs running throughout MSN, Yahoo! and Aol properties. The participating technology companies estimate that millions of people will view the 4 week campaign from the participating companie's sites alone.

"The support of leading technology companies such as microsoft, Yahoo! And aol couldn't have come at a better time. The world wide web has demonstrated that information can be transmitted across america within seconds – and every two seconds some one in America needs a blood transfusion," said Marsha Johnson Evans, President and CEO, american red cross. " our cgoal with this campaign is to significantly increase awareness about the importnace of giving blood now and for a lifetime."

Even though over half of americans are eligible to give blood, only 5 percent actually donate, leaving the nation's supply vulnerable at between a 1 –to 3-day supply. In the interest of National Public Health and Security, the red cross and it's blood bank partners encourage all eligible Americans to help build a safe and stable blood supply 365 days-a-year. Everyday. 34,000 donations are needed to help save the lives of cancer patients, accident victims, and children with blood disorders.

"Microsoft has had a long-standing relationship with the american red cross, from donating software and consulting time and aid in the September 11th relief efforts to providing technology resources year-round that makes chapters across the country more efficient in strengthening there local communities," said

Steve Ballmer, president and CEO, Microsoft Corp. "We are proud to extend our support to include MSN in this public awareness campaign."

"Yahoo! Is pleased to join forces with the american red cross, Aol and Microsoft to raise awareness about this very important national issue," said Terry Semel, chairman and CEO of Yahoo! Inc. "Through this interactive campaign, we are empowering our audience to help save lives by connecting them with ways to give blood."

"Aol is very excited about the opportunity to use our distinct Online programming and community-building features to help our 35 million members learn about the vital importance of blood donation and how he or she can help," said Jonathan Miller, chairman and CEO of America Online, Inc. "Aol is honored to continue to help the red cross extend it's 'Together We Can Save a Life' campaign to the online world."

The internet serves as the premier example of how advances in business and communications technology can bring significant, life changing benefits to those in need. This campaign makes the best use of technology by allowing Online users a convenient offline means to save a life several times a year.

American red cross is working closely with the blood banking community to provide opportunities for donors nationwide to give blood. To schedule an appointment at a blood drive near you, call;

> American red cross at 1-800-GIVE-LIFE
>
> America's Blood Centers at 1-888-USBLOOD
>
> American Association of Blood Banks at 1-866-From-You

The american red cross provides nearly half of the nation's blood supply (collecting more than six million units a year from volunteer donors) to patients in 3,000 hospitals across the country through it's national network. Every 2 seconds, someone in America needs blood. The red cross must collect blood donations each and every day to meet the needs of accident victims, cancer patients and children with blood disorders and works to accomplish this through it's 36 Blood Services regions. Please call today to make your appointment to give the gift of life. Log on to http://blood.givelife.org or call 1-800-GIVE-LIFE to schedule your donation or to sponsor a blood drive.

# Chapter 14
# Legal and Ethical Concerns

## Introduction

The First Amendment to the Constitution provides for freedom of speech, but there are a number of limitations on just how free a media writer's speech can actually be. Libel laws, broadcast regulations, and copyright law all involve limitations of one sort or another on a writer's freedom to publish material. Libel laws are meant to protect someone from being defamed through the media. Broadcast regulations are meant to help achieve fairness and accuracy on the limited number of frequencies available to the media. Copyright law is meant to protect a writer from having his or her words stolen by someone else.

Ethics are also an important concern to a media writer. What is considered ethical or unethical behavior varies from medium to medium and is different for advertisers and public relations practitioners than for newspaper or broadcast journalists.

## Key points

- Media writers should know the First Amendment.

- You must have a strong legal defense if you defame someone.

- Truth, privilege, public/private persons, and fair comment are important defenses.

- Commercial speech has a different level of First Amendment protections.

- Many ethical issues revolve around the appearance of the writer's having a conflict of interest.

- Copyright protections are automatic, but your copyright can be registered with the Copyright Office.

**Here are some useful websites** for more information on legal and ethical concerns in mass communications:

http://www.poynter.org
http://www.asne.org
http://www.splc.org (This site links to the Student Press Law Center, a long-time advocate for student journalists.)
http://www.studentpress.org

## Activity 14.1

Write a short news feature about the following information. Be careful because there is at least one instance of libel below.

There's a new photography teacher at Harbinger Junior College.

Her name is Michelle Motichka and she just finished her doctoral courses at Michigan State University. She is 29 and worked as a photojournalist for Going Places magazine, the publication of the American Automotive Association (AAA) and for the Lubbock Avalanche-Journal.

"I think that I can help instruct young people in how to tell a story with photos. I will make sure that they know the basics of photography, but this is a basic that gets ignored all too frequently.

Dean Peter Seminick is happy to have Motichka aboard. "I know that she will help us get past last semester's problems."

She replaces Harley White, who frequently left the photo lab locked during class time and open lab hours, according to Seminick. "He would come to the office just reeking of booze," Seminick said. "It's sad because he was once a talented teacher, but those days are long gone. He's a lush."

Motichka won a national honorable mention five years for her feature photograph series on rodeo clowns.

The HJC department also suffered last semester when two professors in the American Studies department were arrested in an Internet pornography sting. There are 11 professors in the American Studies department.

As an undergraduate, Motichka was an All-Big Ten golfer, finishing third in the conference as a sophomore. Motichka is 5-foot-8 with blue eyes and light brown hair cut in a shag. She wears oval gold wire-framed glasses.

Said second-year HJC student Taralyn MacCauley: "it's a relief coming here and actually getting instruction. Michelle really helps us understand what photography's all about. She will work with students, instead of telling them that their work sucks."

Said Avalanche-Journal photography editor Ray Hensley: "Michelle was the best photographer out of school we've ever had. I just wish we could have kept her here. She had a knack of getting people in the perfect light."

Said HJC professor Chris Nolan: "We have needed someone with Michelle's ability for quite some time. The photos in the school paper and magazine are 100 times better already."

## Activity 14.2

Write an anniversary story of a major legal finding within your field. You should use Info Trac College Edition as your research tool to find about such important areas as libel cases, the influence of the Federal Communication Commission, or the development of Federal Trade Commission regulation of advertising.

Be sure to treat this story as a news feature for a newsletter or magazine in your field geared toward working professionals. Interview journalism professors or working professionals about the importance of these decisions.

# Activity 14.3

This exercise tests your ability to spot libelous statements in print. For each of the following sentences, decide whether it is libelous or not, assuming the underlined portion of the sentences are provably false.

1. The police arrested Robert Stauffer, 1616 Midkiff Lane, for <u>murdering a convenience store clerk</u>.

2. Ben Drawdy <u>received the team's Most Valuable Player award</u>.

3. Jackson's decline came about three years later when he suffered from <u>the effects of syphilis</u>.

4. <u>A California man committed treasonous acts 30 years ago</u>.

5. <u>Former football star O.J. Simpson stands accused of two charges of assault on a Florida golf course</u>.

6. <u>Actor Sean Penn spent the night in jail after punching out an off-duty policeman</u>.

7. <u>Actor Pauly Shore's performance reminds one of the elementary-school talent show without the cuteness. Or the talent, come to think of it. He's the worst performer on screen ever</u>.

Now assume the following sentences are provably true. Decide whether the sentence is libelous or not.

8. Winthorp suffers from a rare disease that causes him to lose weight despite eating tens of thousands of calories a day. He is truly a starving glutton.

9. Howard cheated the company out of millions of dollars which he then spent in a wild gambling spree on the Internet before going out and contracting a sexually transmitted disease.

10. Norsworthy stole the money.

11. Two of the eight mechanics at Del's Garage have been arrested for their role in a chop-shop near Pasadena.

## Activity 14.4

Using Info Trac College Edition as your research tool, find an example of an ethical question within your field of study.  In a 2-page paper, you should:

A) define the issue
B) list whatever particulars you can find
C) discuss how you would deal with the controversy

# Appendix C
# Media Careers: Ready for Anything

## Introduction

Experience is the key to finding a job in mass communications fields. If you haven't already begun to gather material for your portfolio, the time to begin is now. Take advantage of campus publications or their equivalents in public relations and advertising to begin to collect material. It is also advisable to seek internships with professional organizations - or, at least, it's advisable to try and work part-time for those organizations. To repeat: the diploma just isn't enough in modern mass media.

## Key points

- Professionals expect to see that you can produce professional work.

- Clips from campus publications or equivalents are a start, but one cannot underestimate the value of succeeding at an internship.
- In mass communication jobs, the applicant pool is larger than only specialized majors. The more skills you have, the more employable you may be. This is especially true for developing Internet-related skills.

- Joining student organizations related to mass communication can help show employers that you care about the field.

**And here are some websites** that you may find useful for information on jobs in the media-writing field:

http://www.spj.org (The Society of Professional Journalists' site)

http://www.prsa.org (The Public Relations Society of America's site)

http://www.aaaa.org (The American Association of Advertising Agencies' site)

http://www.ajr.com (The American Journalism Review site)

http://epclassifieds.com (The classified pages of Editor & Publisher)

http://ww.jaws.org/jobs (The Journalism and Women Symposium)

http://www.dowjones.com/newsfund.college (The site for the highly competitive Dow Jones Newspaper Fund internships)

CPSIA information can be obtained
at www.ICGtesting.com
Printed in the USA
FFOW01n2048080914
7282FF